ROMANIANS AND HUNGARIANS

HISTORICAL PREMISES

C. Sassu

ROMANIANS
AND HUNGARIANS

HISTORICAL PREMISES

The Center for Romanian Studies

Las Vegas ◊ Chicago ◊ Palm Beach

Published in the United States of America by
Histria Books
7181 N. Hualapai Way, Ste. 130-86
Las Vegas, NV 89166 USA
HistriaBooks.com

The Center for Romanian Studies is an independent academic and cultural institute with the mission to promote knowledge of the history, literature, and culture of Romania in the world. The publishing program of the Center is affiliated with Histria Books. Contributions from scholars from around the world are welcome. To support the work of the Center for Romanian Studies, contact us at info@centerforromanianstudies.com

Original edition "Cugetarea" — P. Georgescu Delafras, 1940

Library of Congress Control Number: 2021949607

ISBN 978-1-59211-131-2 (hardcover)
ISBN 978-1-59211-198-5 (softbound)
ISBN 978-1-59211-264-7 (eBook)

Contents

Preface

From 1919 until the present day, through innumerable articles in the newspapers and periodicals of various countries, of pamphlets, lectures, maps, statistics, tables, and in general by all the means which active and tireless propaganda can use or think of, endeavors are being made to make the public opinion of the world believe that when certain of the present frontiers in the Danubian basin were fixed, mistakes fatal for the peace and security of Europe had been made. These mistakes are supposed to have produced a state of unbalance so great that, being obviously inconsistent with the natural, geographical, ethnical, historical, and economic conditions of these regions, with their cultural development and with logic and equity, the recommencement of normal life in those parts is an utter impossibility.

The natural consequence of those mistakes is said to be chaos, political anarchy sprung up in the very center of the European continent and producing there Balkan situations akin to those in Macedonia before the war.

So that the maintenance and perpetuation of the present frontiers would constitute a real outrage against civilization, peace, and the normal possibilities of evolution of the whole of Europe.

Economic crises, political tensions, and the confusions which have been disturbing mankind during the twentieth century are said to be due to a great extent to those frontiers considered artificial because by them consolidated unities had been destroyed. Also, that the marking of these boundaries had been achieved by compulsion and by surprise; by compulsion because impossible conditions had been imposed on an adversary who did not have the right to protest or explain, and by catching unawares well-meaning statesmen who however were entirely ignorant of the real situation in those regions.

It is being affirmed that only in such circumstances was it possible to commit against Hungary — in a moment of tragic surprise — so crying an injustice, with consequences so damaging for the whole of the civilized world.

Impressed by the perseverance with which that thesis is being ceaselessly upheld under different forms in conformity with the political necessities of the moment, I have tried to analyze the bases of those affirmations when applied to a concrete case.

As the relations between Romania and Hungary are continually being disturbed by that propaganda action, it is to the interest of both states and to that of the maintenance of peace in the Danubian basin, that the belief should not take root that persistently repeated affirmations can be accepted as truths merely by their simple repetition. This little book limiting itself to the historical premises of Romanian-Hungarian relations tries to explain as lucidly as possible the real value of the affirmations made, in the hope that minds unbiased by passion and not narrowed by self-interest will think it useful and opportune to know the true elements of a controversy, which is being carried on with such ostentation and presented as being one of the great unsolved political problems of the age in which we live.

Romanians and Hungarians
Historical Premises

The statement that in order to understand political phenomena it is absolutely necessary to be acquainted with their historical setting is less contested today than ever before because the influence of those phenomena is directly felt to be decisive, on collective as well as personal destinies.

Hence, it is acknowledged that only in the perspective of time can the true and specific significance of contemporary events be understood. That is the reason we have been witnessing for some years that rich effluence of historical studies and romanced histories, all corresponding to the unanimous wish of finding a guiding thread and an intelligible explanation for the chaotic appearance of the tragic events which succeeded one another with such great rapidity.

Following that general inclination, alleged historical arguments occupy a front place also among the motives invoked to obtain a change in the present political situation of the Danubian basin.

Hence, the image of a "millennial Hungary" is constantly being evoked, which is supposed to have formed over the centuries the best guarantee of balance and stability, of peace, prosperity, and progress of those so excessively sensitive regions, in the very center of the European continent.

I

Hungarian Revisionism

Only as a result of the unavoidable opposition which the anachronism of forming again a "millennial Hungary" meets all the time in the responsible quarters of the various states, conscious of the danger which the total and wished for overturning of the existing states in such obvious contradiction to ethnical facts would present, of the fatal and immediate political repercussions which those changes would have for all the countries of the civilized world, has the absurd claim of asking for the complete remaking of Hungary in her so-called millennial frontiers been renounced for the time being for tactical and opportune motives.

A more realistic calculation of the circumstances showed that for the attainment of that final purpose it would be far better to proceed in stages, to limit for the time being — per the suggestions made by Stephen Bethlen — the absurd claims to the following three points:

1. Retrocession, without a plebiscite, of the regions along the frontiers of neighboring states which are said to be inhabited by a Hungarian population.

2. A plebiscite in Banat and Bacica.

3. Independence of Transylvania.

An objective examination of the historical evolution will show to what extent those claims are based on facts and to what extent their satisfaction is to the general interest of more natural and fairer order in the center of the European continent.

II

Did "Millennial Hungary" Exist?

Looked at in this way any unbiased observer establishes a first and preliminary fact concerning the initial premise on which the political claims are based, namely that "millennial Hungary" so often invoked is nothing but a fiction invented by historiography and by the Hungarian State's official jurists and is unconfirmed by historical facts. As everyone knows, the Hungarian "Apostolic Kingdom" founded by Stephen I under the patronage of the Holy See, through his coronation on 15 August 1001 with a crown sent to him by Pope Sylvester the Second, ceased to exist on 29 August 1526 after a stormy life which lasted five centuries, having collapsed in the catastrophic battle of Mohács under the merciless attack of the Turks, who were then at the height of their power during the glorious reign of Sultan Suleiman II, surnamed the Magnificent. That decisive defeat was followed shortly after by the conquest of Buda (1529) and the transformation of Hungary proper into a Turkish pashalik. (1541).

The remnants of the former Hungarian Kingdom were then divided up between Archduke Ferdinand, brother of Charles V and his deputy in the Empire, as well as the brother-in-law of Louis II, last King of Hungary, who had fallen on the battlefield of Mohács, and John Zápolya, Voivode of Transylvania. The Archduke occupied the territories bordering on the countries which were under the Habsburg rule, and John Zápolya took over the Eastern parts, the Sultan conferring on him "a kingdom which belonged to the victor of Mohács by the right of war and the sword."

From that date until the Peace of Karlowitz (1699), the Porte ruled in the place of the Hungarian State in the Pannonian plain. For a century and a half these territories were governed by a Turkish pasha who resided in Buda, formerly the residential city of the kings of Hungary, just as in Banat, a little further South, another pasha held sway.

At the end of the seventeenth century, when the "Eastern Question" was born as a result of the weakening of the Ottoman Empire and when the generals of Leopold I, the Emperor in Vienna, conquered Hungary with the sword, Christian domination was reestablished in these regions as well, but nevertheless remained totally foreign to them.

Beginning from 1699, the year in which the Karlowitz Peace was signed and until the middle of the nineteenth century, Hungary and Transylvania, which had been acquired at the same time using threats and pressures, constituted two distinct provinces similar to all the others in the extensive Hapsburg monarchy, each having its own juridical and administrative forms in conformity with local traditions.

It was only recently, from 1867 to the end of World War I, that Hungary managed to include Transylvania within its borders and to reconstitute itself, for a period of 51 years, into an autonomous state within the Hapsburg monarchy, transformed into the Dual Monarchy.

III

Can the Invocation of a
"Millennial Hungary" Constitute
an Argument for Revisionism?

So that in lieu of the so often invoked "millennial Hungary" there existed six different dominations — for during the period in between 1526, 1541 and 1699 three parallel dominations must be reckoned: the Imperial one, the Turkish one, and the Transylvanian one under the sovereignty of the Turks; the ephemeral revolutionary creations of a later period, namely that of Francis Rákoczi II (1703-1711) and Louis Kossuth (1848-1849) need not be taken into account — held sway on territories said to be and claimed as integral parts of a state which has not had and could not have, as is obvious, anything but the value of an ideological fiction, for there can be no possible question under such circumstances of a real continuity of the state's existence.

It is of course natural that some connecting elements should have existed between these different dominations on the same territories, but it is just as certain that they differed profoundly in character and significance. Hence to claim territories which at some time or other were subjected to any of those past dominations, without being able to base those claims on incontestable ethnical arguments is as little justified as if, for instance, France would lay claim today to territories which formed part of Charlemagne's Empire, or Great Britain would ask of France the provinces which once belonged to her kings, or if Germany and Spain demanded from Italy the provinces over which they had ruled in the Peninsula, or again if Sweden claimed from Prussia the regions which she had taken from her in the past.

The absurdity of any such claim in the cases enumerated above for purposes of comparison is obvious because the facts and the historical circumstances which caused them are well-known in all countries; but if we examine more closely the circumstances connected with the claims put forward by Hungarian revisionism, we shall see that these claims are equally unjustified.

IV

The Origin, Character, and Penetration of the Hungarians into the Pannonian Plain Condition the Frontiers of Present-Day Hungary

So, coming back to the conditions which contributed in that historical moment to the foundation of the Hungarian state by King Stephen I, we see that neither the determining factors nor the object for which it was created could confer on it the character of a national state, but merely that of a Christian medieval state in the Western Catholic sense. The establishing of that fact does not minimize the personal qualities of the first king; on the contrary, it reveals his political intuition which, realizing the favorable circumstances of the moment, overcame the ethnical and geographical premises and succeeded in transforming the rudimentary collectivity of the Hungarian tribes into a connected organism of the state, able to play an important role in the Danubian basin. To be able to appreciate both the importance and the real scope and character of his state creation, we must remember that the Hungarians were one of those peoples that have been swept by the migration surge that characterized the end of the Roman Empire and of Greek-Latin civilization from out-of-the-way regions outside the European geographical horizon of those times, into the intensely civilized centers of the Ancient World.

Linguistic research leads us to believe that the Hungarians have sprung from the Finno-Ugric, tribes originating in the Ural Mountains, who, having suffered in the Caucasus region under the influence of the Western Turku-Ugric, ancestors of the early Bulgarians, occupied in the ninth century the extensive, pasture land in Southern Russia. Attacked in the regions along the river Don by the Pechenegs, another nomad people, they were compelled to divide themselves up into two unequal parts. The smaller part having been driven towards the Volga disappeared, absorbed by the Tartars and other steppe tribes; the larger half, composed of seven tribes which were joined by three Turkish-speaking tribes, settled temporarily in Etelkus, in the Southern region between the Prut and the Dniester. Thence the Hungarian tribes made innumerable incursions into neighboring countries until they were compelled in 896, as a result of an unexpected attack on two sides — by the Pechenegs and by the Bulgarians — to leave their dwellings and, led by Arpad, son of Almash, chief of one of their leading tribes (the Magyar tribe), whom they made a hereditary prince, they turned as the Huns had done before them towards the fertile plains of old Pannonia, situated between the rivers Tisa, Danube and Drava. They knew of these places through an invasion made into Moravia a few years before.

Their coming to these parts had not yet the character of a definite settlement and could quite easily have remained nothing but an incident, as temporary and ephemeral as had been the dominations of other nomad peoples. Neither their number nor the geographical conditions nor their state of culture could give them perspectives of duration or allow them to foresee the lucky historical opportunity which gave them the possibility of finding their setting in the political system of the epoch in a manner so favorable to themselves.

As regards the number of the Hungarians who came to those parts, it could certainly not be greater than that of other migrating nomad tribes of that period, who, cut off from their homeland or kin-tribes, were only able to form lonely oases amid the other civilized peoples and, as a consequence, were not in a position to establish durable state institutions.

Nevertheless, the Hungarians had great luck, as compared to other peoples who were in a similar situation, to find Pannonia, owing to repeated invasions and barbarian dominations, only very sparsely populated, even when compared to the usual sparseness of the population in the majority of European countries during the Middle Ages, where extensive areas were still covered with forests. That is how the Hungarians in Pannonia escaped from being absorbed by the native population which was superior to them from a cultural point of view. The proof is that in the Hungarian language the words referring to trades, institutions, and civilized notions are, as a general rule, of Slavic origin.

That sparseness of the native population enabled the Hungarians to arrange their settlements in Pannonia according to tribes, on large areas, in the manner of a nomad people accustomed to wide spaces and extensive plains.

For it was that very characteristic of open plain which fitted their mode of life so well and the absence of impassable boundaries that might have prevented their frequent incursions into neighboring countries and even further, which made them settle in Pannonia.

Hence, it is proven that one of the motives most insistently invoked to obtain today a modification of the present frontiers in favor of Hungary, namely the alleged drawback of not having any natural geographical boundaries, was the very cause and primordial reason why the Hungarians settled in Pannonia in the very territory enclosed by the boundaries fixed at the peace of Trianon, contested with such vehemence.

From this Pannonian territory which the first Hungarian chroniclers of the twelfth to the fourteenth centuries describe as being inhabited at the Hungarians' coming by Sclavi, Bulgari, *ac pastores Romanorum* also described as Blahi, *qui et olim fuerunt Romanorum pastores*, the Hungarians continued their customary incursions into almost all the countries of Europe, constituting a permanent danger for most of the countries of that time. Their invasions however were directed by preference towards the West.

Making use of that very absence of impassable boundaries, and more especially of that opening which the region of depression around Vienna forms, the so-called Porta Hungarica, situated between the Bohemian range — the chief natural fortress in the north of the Danubian basin — and the Alpine countries, their predatory expeditions spread terror and misery in Bavaria, Medieval Saxony, Swabia, France, and Italy.

In the tenth century, Western Europe lived in constant dread of the Hungarian invasions, until finally Henry I and Otto I, by their famous victories at Merseburg (933) and Augsburg (955), cut them off from the heart of Europe.

V

History, Character, and Privileged Structure of the Hungarian Apostolic Kingdom of the Middle Ages

Only a happy chance because Otto I was too taken up with other problems, such as the subjugation and Germanizing of the Slavs, East of the Elbe, and the expeditions into Italy to obtain his future imperial dignities, saved the Hungarians from being completely annihilated and having the same fate as their kinsmen, the Huns and the Avars.

In opposition to them, like an advanced bastion of Western civilization, Emperor Otto I formed anew the Marca Ostica, laying thus the foundation of future Austria and the German preponderance in the Danubian basin.

All these events, however, did not fail to leave lasting traces, for settling in the neighborhood of consolidated Germanism, the Hungarian people were henceforth subjected to its continually growing influence and to that of the Christian culture which it represented. Under that influence, it was compelled to give up the nomadic life which it had been leading and, abandoning its tribal existence, to give to the collectivity a large consistency, adopting the political, social, and cultural forms of the medieval Western World. Their atavistic nomad instincts manifested until then in constant invasions became transformed into a well-defined tendency to expand, more especially towards the South-

East, where, the situation being still confused, the opposition was easier to overcome.

These tendencies were definitely adopted and realized during the reign of Stephen I (1001-1038). For that reason, just as his father had done before him, Stephen I encouraged foreigners, especially Germans, to settle in the country and granted them a favored régime, so that with their aid he would be able to consolidate his monarchical power and defeat the particularist resistances of the tribes. He likewise needed their help to exterminate both the rooted paganism and the Christian Orthodox faith which the Hungarians had begun to accept from the native population they had found in Pannonia, namely from those "Slavs and Roman shepherds" mentioned by the Chroniclers. The king's political intuition made him recognize in Catholicism the dominant force of the times with the help of which he could change the national Hungarian collectivity into a missionary territorial state.

The title of "Apostolic King" obtained from Rome with a royal crown, consecrated that deep transformation. That title defines the character of the new state and shows in a symbolical formula, both its factors of power and ascension, as well as its elements of weakness.

In truth, the apostolic kingdom came into being in an epoch when the Western World, living in the nightmare of waiting for the expected end of the world and Day of Judgement, wished to atone by acts of faith for the original sin in order to be able to enjoy eternal bliss. At that time, born of that ardent wish of salvation, the thought of a crusade against unbelievers and heretics took shape for the first time in the mind of Pope Sylvester II.

With the desired crusade in view, the Pope even consented to uphold the Utopian scheme of Emperor Otto III, his former disciple, in whose veins flowed both the blood of his German ancestors, who looked upon themselves as the descendants of Charlemagne and that of the Byzantine emperors. Wishing to rebuild, in a new Catholic-Christian form, the old Roman empire in its entirety, Otto III planned a confederacy of Catholic states with Rome as its center and under the leadership of himself and the Pope. The conferring by the Emperor of the title of patrician on Duke Boleslav of Poland and the Apostolic Crown by the Pope on the future King Stephen I of Hungary, was to be the first step in the realization of that vast project of collecting the whole Christian world into a strange unity, conceived after the model of the empire as a federation of Catholic sovereigns. The premature death of the two prominent initiators prevented the continuation on those lines of that unlimited medieval imperialism which tended, though not taking into consideration ethnic facts and given possibilities, to enthrone the universal uncontested domination of empire in the hierarchical forms of the feudal state.

Allies, for the time being, the two influential factors of the medieval world, the Empire and the Papacy, were each shortly to follow their plans of universal hegemony fighting openly, one against the other, and thus to provoke the fall of the entire medieval system.

It was natural that in that fight the Hungarian Apostolic Kingdom should be on the side of Papacy, its kings acknowledging themselves to be, right from the beginning of the thirteenth century, formal vassals of the Holy See. But it was just as natural that this Kingdom, a deliberate political construction of the historical moment, favored but also conditioned, both in its constitutive form and in its possibilities of life and development by the characteristic conditions of the epoch which produced it, should, with the fall of the whole medieval system, lose its very reason for existence. For the "Apostolic Kingdom" disavowed its national character by its very birth certificate, adopting, as did the Crusaders' states of later years, the narrow political and social base and the ideological unilateral premise of the feudal system.

These organic vices were all the more fatal for the evolution of the Hungarian state given the great disproportion which existed between its ethnical possibilities and the political aims which it had fixed for itself.

It was that same fatal disproportion that prevented it from evolving normally, like the other states, by a gradual adaptation of constitutional forms to national realities, forcing it in order to maintain its territorial extension, to preserve under outward changes its initial form in rigid immutability.

The tragic incompatibility between the legal form and the ethical facts forced the king who represented the new form of state to fight, from the very beginning, against the living forces of the nation represented by the Hungarian tribes and their leaders. For the king wished to destroy the primitive community of the Hungarian state, in order to be able to mold it into new constitutional forms similar to those of the West, where historical circumstances had produced, in a process of the slow evolution from the diversity of feudal ties, those small privileged strata superimposed in hierarchical order, which formed the state organization of that time.

In order to be able to fulfill its Catholic missionary aim, the Hungarian state cast away its natural ethnic ties, introducing that process of narrowing its internal foundation and of widening its external domination, which later on was to give to the social and national problems on its territories a catastrophic gravity.

Through being in the service of the Papacy's tendencies toward universal hegemony, which was trying in that epoch to transform Europe into a republic of rules directed by the supreme ecclesiastical authority, the Hungarian kings were able to benefit from the support of the whole Western world, which alone enabled them to change the character of the state they inherited, transforming it into a non-national state of aristocratic construction.

The new state construction realized in the constitutional doctrine of the "Holy Crown" could not conceive of rights except as privileges and recognized no other but members of the "Holy Crown" as elements of the state. And those members of the "Holy Crown" could be no other than the aristocratic corporations created by the king as representing the nation. Representing him on the whole territory of the state, the members of those aristocratic corporations, classified in their turn into a hierarchical order of their own, had even sovereign attributions, exercising all public, military, jurisdictional, administrative, and spiritual functions, and only they had exclusive ownership rights to landed estates, the whole country being considered as a royal domain so that only the king could confer property rights. In this way, with the introduction of individual properties to the advantage of certain privileged sections, the majority of the population was taken out of the framework of the state by the new constitutional order and obliged to remain underlings dependent on certain privileged persons either individual or collective formed into corporations, in the strata from which the organization of state was composed and which limited it. Among those strata which the new forms of right had superimposed on the country like a spiderweb, either in the form of assemblies of nobles or under other forms and territorial institutions, clerics and foreigners played an important part, because they were not hampered by traditional ties, possessed the corresponding spiritual conformation formed by the feudal atmosphere of their native land, and constituted the necessary connecting links with the outside world, the kings relied on. For it was not a nationality but the spiritual conformation, that is to say, the feudal mentality which interested that state, which could not be conceived as being anything but a Catholic and nobiliary organization of a territory as extensive as possible. In the advice which the founder himself, King Stephen I, gave to his son, that thought is expressed in the following words: "a country with one single language and one single lot of customs is weak and fragile."

As a matter of fact, foreign help was also needed to be able to spread the domination over the neighboring countries, as the Hungarian ethnic power was much too weak to be able to keep up that domination in the various geographical unities which were beginning to be added to the native territory of the Hungarian state.

Following unending dynastic fights which weakened the King's power, those strata having succeeded in freeing themselves gradually from the tutorship of the head power which had bestowed on them that privileged situation, formed themselves into autonomous corporations and ruled unhindered over the territories which until then they had held as vassals of the king. So that at the beginning of the Angevin epoch, the Hungarian State appeared to be a federation of territorial corporations of nobles superimposed on the existing population.

Under such conditions, the forced entrance of Hungarian domination into neighboring countries in the name of Catholic missionarism and Christian civilization was, as a matter of fact, determined by much more personal and selfish motives. That extension of domination meant bringing under that same kind of rule of the nobles' large territories and a vast productive population, which could constitute new sources of wealth and a promising means of advancement in the order of privileged hierarchies. That is the reason why the desire for domination has taken such deep root in the conscience of those privileged strata which consider themselves even today as being the real and only representatives of the Hungarian people. The lawsuit of the "optants" which was carried on so vehemently during the years which followed the First World War, revealed anew the motives of a continuous and tenacious action which tried to reconquer, hiding its real intentions under high-sounding slogans like "the sanctity of ownership rights" and "equal national rights", the privileged position which historical development had taken from it.

VI

Geographical Discordances Created through the Penetration of the Hungarian Domination into the Neighboring Countries

With the authority which its missionary aim conferred on it and the superiority which the more perfect military organization of its privileged nobility gave it, the Hungarian Apostolic Kingdom succeeded in roping in the large countries in the neighborhood, amongst which Croatia, Dalmatia, and especially Transylvania are of great importance.

By the subjugation of these countries the "Apostolic Kingdom" became in addition to an artificial construction from the political and social point of view, also a disconnected conglomeration from the geographical and ethnical one. By assembling unities divergent in nature into a state organization in which the only common element in the varied mosaic of the component parts was on the one hand the superimposed hierarchy of the privileged class and on the other, the economic decadence and the unfair political and social treatment of the population, the "Apostolic Kingdom" continued to be in the Danubian basin a center of unending struggles and hence a permanent element of trouble.

The forcing of natural conditions which the territorial extension of the Hungarian kingdom represented is evident when one looks at a map, from which it is obvious that Croatia and Dalmatia are Mediterranean regions with marked tendencies towards the Adriatic and that Transylvania like a natural bastion forms the center of a well-defined geographical unity bounded by the Tisa on the West, by the Dniester on the East, by the Danube on the South and by Maramureş Mountains on the North, the whole of that complex being conditioned and intimately bound to the mouths of the Danube and the Black Sea.

The geographical discordances of medieval Hungary between frontiers widened in this way, made even Count Stephen Szécheny, the founder of the Hungarian Academy, who in his country was considered the greatest Hungarian patriot, despair and exclaim anxiously: "Thou seest, O Lord, that our geographical position is not favorable."

The plateau of Transylvania more especially had a totally incongruous position in connection with the Pannonian plain, the depression of the river Tisa forming until a few decades ago an immense marsh which cut off the Carpathian regions entirely from the other territories of the "Hungarian Apostolic Kingdom", even more effectively than a high range of mountains without openings for travelers, would have done.

VII

Geographical Unity of the Carpathian Region

Compared to that so very abnormal geographical situation of the medieval Hungarian State, the regions around the Carpathian bastion contained between the three boundary rivers Tisa, Dniester, and the Danube, formed both by their system of waters and by the currents of traffic which traversed them, a natural unity so harmonic, so representative of the perfected ethnical unity of the Romanian people who inhabited them, that the Hungarian Kingdom's domination in these parts can only be explained by the historical circumstances of the moment and by the undeveloped state of the political organizations of that epoch.

Rightly the geographical unity of those Carpathian regions has been compared to a natural citadel, "Transylvania and its crown of mountains forming the citadel proper, Tisa and Dniester the moats surrounding the fortress." The not-too-great height of the Transylvanian plateau — about 500 meters — has always made it a good place to live and the many passes which cross the Carpathians established the contact, permitting a continuous and uninterrupted connection to be kept up between the two mountain slopes.

The Romanian people have been linked to that geographical unity since its birth. Like their ancestors, the Dacians, they have often been obliged to "stick close to the mountains" in the valleys and forests which offered shelter, for being situated on the Eastern border of Europe, the Vistula and Dniester constituting the true frontiers of our continent, they stood always in the path of invaders, of all migrations which have accompanied them, for thousands of years, the unending conflict between the Western and the Eastern World. For that reason, it has only been possible with the utmost difficulty to give to these regions — predestined by nature to constitute harmonious organisms of state — powerful political organizations of their own. For these states which were the outmost sentinels of Western civilization, could develop only in times of stability and equilibrium, their very existence being a symptom of the consolidation of order in Europe.

The Romans also recognized the great importance of those regions for the peace and security of Europe. Having succeeded in uniting the whole Mediterranean world into one state and civilization which constitutes the bases of modern culture, they naturally enough devoted special attention to regions so important strategically for the maintenance of their domination in the East. But it was the Greeks who discovered, before them, the economic value of these regions.

VIII

Origin of the Romanian People: Prehistoric Civilization, Thracians and Dacians

So that owing to the favorable living conditions it would seem that the Carpathian territories have been inhabited since times immemorial, even during the Paleolithic age. In the age that followed the neo and Eneolithic periods, those regions formed even — like the traces of painted pottery show — the center of a brilliant civilization, the area of which stretched over the whole southeast of Europe, from the Aegean Sea to the Northern Carpathians and from Pannonia to the region of Kiev.

One of those prehistorical civilizations, namely the "Boian A" civilization, originally from the plain of Wallachia, came to the Transylvanian plateau through the pass in the Ţara Bârsei, proving that even at that far-old epoch the Carpathian Mountains were not an impossible boundary, but an obstacle easy enough to overcome in order to maintain those exchanges of goods which constitute the necessary preliminary conditions for the formation of any unitary civilized sphere.

Concerning which people created that unity of civilization opinions are divided. It would seem however that it must be attributed to the Thracians, that Indo-European people which, coming from the North scattered themselves all over the Balkan Peninsula as far as the Adriatic Sea, in Macedonia, in the Islands of the Aegean Sea, and even in Asia Minor, and close kin to the people that produced the Trojan civilization described in Homer's poems. In the conscience of mankind, the Thracians live through the influence they had over the Greeks, the God Dionysos and his orgiastic cult being one of the determining factors which fostered the birth of the tragic feeling expressed in the imperishable forms of antique tragedy.

The Northern branch of the Thracians were the Dacians or Getae, who lived where Romania is today but on a still larger area, between the Tisa Plain in the West and Crimea in the East, neighbored to the North by kindred nations which stretched as far as Moravia and even over the Carpathians as far as the Vistula and the Baltic Sea.

While the Thracians from South of the Danube turning to the East were conquered by the brilliant Greek and Oriental civilizations, the Dacians, more conservative, inclined to the West, towards Italian and Celtic influences more akin to their nature as tillers of the soil and shepherds. Due to this, it was possible later on, when the victorious Roman empire at the beginning of the second century extended its domination over those regions also and included them in the great civilizing unity of the Mediterranean World, with its universal value and character, to Romanize them completely in a century and a half.

But before they came under the Roman domination, the Dacians had succeeded at different times, by forming powerful political formations, to give unity and consistency to Central Europe.

Their religion which embodied a high idealism and belief in the immortality of the soul proved to be an excellent means of ethnic solidarity, giving them the moral power to fulfill that mission. Indeed, the cult of Zalmoxis, the supreme god of Persian origin, imposed on believers an austere behavior and held out to them the hope of eternal life in the company of the god, through death on the battlefield, which freed the soul from the body and from the impure passions which dominate it.

Hence, the servants of the god were highly respected, so that advice given by the priest had the value of a real divine command. With their help, the kings who came from among the nobles rich in lands, belonging to the autonomous tribes in the time of patriarchal organizations, succeeded in extending their authority over the large Dacian territories populated with villages perched on heights difficult of access, and in forming political unities as powerful as were the kingdoms of Burebista and Decebal.

IX

The Roman-Dacian conflict

The kingdom of the first preoccupied even Caesar who had not his tragic death cut him off from life prematurely, intended to undertake an expedition against the Dacians, for already then Roman imperialism on its way towards the East knocked against the expansive power of Burebista's state along the Danube and in the Balkans.

So that Trajan's wars with Decebal were just the last episodes of the dramatic conflict full of vicissitudes, which had divided the two peoples for over two centuries, and which kept growing in intensity in proportion with the progress made by Roman domination in those parts.

As a result of the extension of Roman domination as far as the middle Danube, during the reign of Octavian Augustus, the Dacians, caught as in a vice, made under Decebal one last serious effort to organize in the Transylvanian plateau a powerful center, capable of mobilizing all elements of resistance against Roman domination. At first, it even seemed that the effort had chances of success, for the great offensive begun against Dacia by Emperor Domitian ended in a painful failure, the Romans being compelled to make peace with Decebal in the year 82 A.D., obliging themselves to pay him an annual sum, send him experts for the military constructions he needed and provide him with various engines of war.

It was natural that Trajan's tireless perseverance and his far-sighted care should not be able to tolerate the perpetuation of a situation which, as he realized very well, had greatly damaged Roman prestige. There were also the dangers presented by the existence of an independent Dacian state at the mouths of the Danube, in a spot so strategically important due to the dominating situation it had been given by nature in the Danubian basin and in the Balkan Peninsula, which could be used as an entrance gate for any enemy attack against the Eastern provinces of the European empire.

Despite unlimited resources and exceptional preparations, the Dacian's heroic resistance could only be overcome by Trajan after two terrible and bloody fights, and after several years of efforts from 101 − 102 to 105 − 106, when the last opposition was broken at Sarmizegetusa, the mighty, mysterious and almost inaccessible bastion on the summits close to the present little town of Orăştie, in the Southwest of Transylvania.

X

Thracian and Roman Succession

With the subjugation of Dacia and its transformation into a Roman province, disappeared the last attempt in antiquity to give the Danubian basin a political organization of its own. Henceforth for a long time to come, these regions were to be just annexes of other political systems.

The Dacians' history, however, does not end with the disappearance of the state but continues in the regions bordering the new province making itself felt often through the numerous incursions made into the interior of the Roman province by the Dacians in those parts, usually in company with other peoples. The memory of the Dacians however has remained and is even kept alive today through deeper and more living traces than the narratives of ancient authors or archaeological remains. That memory has been kept up in a great many toponymical names such for instance the names of the Carpathian Mountains, the rivers Danube, Someş, Olt, Mureş, Tisa, Motru, Argeş, and Buzău, of Abrud in Transylvania, not far from the Western frontier of the Romania of today. It lives in a great many customs of the Romanian people whose ethnic bases were the Dacians, in their chief occupations of tillers of the soil and shepherds, in the way they build their houses with beams covered with clay, in the dress and blood of the Romanian peasant, in his way of going about bareheaded and allowing his hair to grow, in the shirts worn outside the trousers and tied round the waist, in the trousers fitting tight over the ankles, in the woolen weaving and deft embroideries, in the peasant art, a result of ancestral inheritance, in the close connection of the tiller with the soil, but above all in the whole nation's power of endurance and resistance which despite all hardships remained through the centuries for thousands of years in the places which had belonged to it at the beginning.

But the romanity of the Romanian people, expressed by its language, by its characteristic folklore, and by the superior spiritual forms embodied in its culture, was the deliberately planned work of Emperor Trajan, whose personality lives even today in the consciences of the peoples of these regions, in the legendary forms of the Romanian and Balkan Slav folklore.

XI
The Romanization of the Dacians

The Romanizing of Dacia was effected at an exceptionally rapid and intensive pace immediately after the conquest of Dacia. For the Romanizing of Dacia was the chief problem which filled the whole reign of the Emperor rightly called "Optimus princeps" by the Italian scholar Roberto Paribeni, that is to say, the leader in which were embodied in the most complete degree the qualities of the sovereign, in the sense of the first servant of the state caring for its vital and permanent interests.

His longing to conquer Dacia being so great that he was wont to end any promise with the oath "so help me God to see Dacia changed into a Roman province", Emperor Trajan, whose reign is also the apogee of Roman power, he being the last emperor who succeeded "to plant the Roman eagles on lands as yet untrodden by the legions", began the remaking and Romanizing of Dacia according to a well-conceived plan long since prepared in every detail.

Predestined it would seem by his provincial origin, by his Italian-Spanish blood, for that grand work, he was also familiar through his own experience, as Governor of Germany, with the colonization methods of Rome, so perfected by an experience of many centuries.

So that once Dacia had been subjugated, Trajan was able to take immediately all necessary measures to transform as rapidly as possible that advanced bastion in the barbarian world — which his military genius had recognized as being of immense importance for the maintenance of Roman peace — into a country completely Roman. For the Emperor realized perfectly well that only a very rapid Romanization could protect Dacia against the growing aggressiveness of the barbarians. For that reason, the Emperor created in Dacia, from the very moment of conquest, the needful conditions for the active inclusion of the country in the field of the empire's economic interests and for the beginning of an intensive Roman life which was to catch in its superior civilized forms the native population of the conquered Dacians, accustomed to the patriarchal life of their rustic tradition.

For that purpose, he organized the new province after the manner in which the most Romanized provinces had been organized.

Bringing over — as Eutropius points out — "unending crowds" of colonists "from the whole Roman world", but more especially from the neighboring and Romanized Illyricum, Emperor Trajan and his successors laid the undestroyable ethnic foundation of the Romanity of these regions and by a good administrative organization and a prosperous economic state they gave the country the possibilities to enjoy all the advantages of Roman peace in the second century of the Christian era, "of peace and prosperity within the protecting limes."

The building of several flourishing towns as were, for example, Ulpia Trajana Augusta, the unsuspected size of which was brought to light by the archaeological excavations made within the last ten years by Romanian scholars, and Porolissum in the North of Transylvania, now being excavated, and many others; the making of high roads, those famous Roman roads which have given to the natural ways for trade a new life and to the population the feeling of perfect security, increased also by a perfected system of arranging the camps and garrisons as well as the protective trenches, testify to the grandeur of the work accomplished and prove that the name of "Happy Dacia." conferred on the country during that time, was not an empty epithet but that in truth the conscious will of its Imperial founder had succeeded in guiding a country and a people towards a new destiny.

XII

Dacia in the Epoch of Migrations: The Slavs and the Formation of the Romanian People's Individuality

The great social, political and economic crisis which shook to its bases the Roman Empire during the following century, changing its character and weakening its powers of resistance against the more and more rabid attacks of the surrounding barbarian tribes, provoked in Dacia also a fall in the level of civilization by relapsing into former states of rustic primitiveness. The exposed position of the province forced Emperor Aurelian to withdraw the Roman legions and administration between 271 and 275 A.D. and to fix the new frontiers of the Empire at the Danube, on a short line easier to protect.

In this way Dacia came under the successive rule of the barbarians who invaded Europe, and more especially Southern Europe, beginning with the third century. Their stay in Dacia, however, merely constituted a stage in their rush towards the civilized centers of the Roman world, towards Constantinople and Italy, which were the real aims of their desires.

Through the disappearance of the old forms of state, the process of formation of the Romanian people begun in Dacia by the Roman colonization became slower and was hindered to a certain extent by the unfavorable conditions. But at the same time, that process was amplified by the inclusion of other national elements into the technical unity of the Romanian people.

Of these, the most important one was the Slavs, whose influence is testified in the language by the large number of words which they left, the institutions of collective organization, both political and social, and in the spiritual, cultural, and liturgical forms of the Romanian people.

Nevertheless, the Slavic, the influence was not sufficiently strong to spoil the Romanian people's original Dacian-Roman blood, which is proved both by the physical appearance and the spiritual structure, by the expressions used for fundamental notions, by the words most frequently used, by the Latin morphology and syntax of the language, by the individualist conscience and the rationalist sharpness of character.

So that it may be affirmed with truth "that the Romanians are a Romanic people with a Slav strain just as the French, Italians, and Spaniards are Romanic people with a Germanic strain." Consequently, amid the large Romanic family the Romanians represent "a peculiar characteristic variation and a unique possibility of civilization" corresponding to their peculiar geographical position, like an island isolated among peoples of another race.

For another result of the Slav migration was the breaking up of the Thracian-Latin territorial continuity in the Eastern parts of the Empire, where extensive territories were lost to Romanity by the settling in masses of the Slavs and the denationalizing of the native population.

In Dacia, the phenomenon was inverted, because when the Slavs came the process of Romanization was more advanced and the majority of the Slavs were driven forward over the Danube, nearer to their desired aims, by the barbarian hordes pressing impatiently forward from the rear. There is no doubt but that the land conformation, the Carpathian plateau with its sheltered valleys and huge forests, favored the conservation of the Romanian people who, after the declining of civilization during the last decades of the Roman domination, having returned gradually to the rustic life of their ancestral tradition, could adapt themselves more easily to the harsh conditions of life created by the new circumstances.

For at the coming of the invading waves, the Dacian population fled and took shelter both in the natural citadel of the mountains and in the immense forests on hill and plain, reappearing as a perfect unitary nation to reoccupy the territories it had had, as soon as those waves had died down somewhat and an organized life had again become possible.

It was in those sheltered places under the threat of the common danger represented by the invasions coming from the East and by the dominations resulting therefrom that the Romanians lived side by side with the Slavs, a few tribes of whom first appeared in Dacia after the departure of the Goths and the conversion to Christianity of the native Dacian-Roman population.

Obliged to pay the tribute in kind demanded by those foreign masters, the two producing populations, the Dacian-Romans, and the Slavs drew nearer and influenced one another until the stronger vitality of the natives prevailed. That step in their development was marked by their acceptance of the ecclesiastical organization of the Slavicized Bulgarian State which, as a result of the missionary work of the apostles Methodius and Cyril, was on the way to win over to the Eastern Orthodox Church the whole Danubian basin.

XIII

Primitive Slavic-Romanian Voivodates; the Beginnings of Some Autochthonous Political Organizations

The Dacian-Romans, having completed their ethnic individualization by the absorption of the Slavic population and become Romanians, even succeeded in creating a few small collective communities.

These primitive formations adapted to local needs and patriarchal conditions were called "cnezate" if small and "voivodeships" if large. Several "cnezate" formed a voivodeship.

Although in the beginning, these voivodeships were usually limited to not too extensive and sparsely populated districts, put under the authority of a chosen leader whose duty it was to deal out justice in peace time and to command in war time, they were nevertheless capable of becoming, as had the former kingdoms of their Dacian forefathers, serious state formations on an autochthonous basis, to represent and uphold the political interests of the unitary geographical region surrounding the Carpathian bastion.

If that development could have been possible, the enthronement of order based on a sensible balancing of the natural factors in the Danubian basin would also have become possible.

XIV

The Part Played in History by the Voivodates of Wallachia and Moldavia; Michael the Brave and the Rebuilding of the National Unity of the Carpathian Region

For the entire history of the Wallachian and Moldavian principalities, which have sprung from those voivodeships — the state formations characteristic of the Romanian people for several centuries, namely from the fourteenth to the middle of the nineteenth century — is characterized by that very constant tradition to eliminate, as far as possibilities and the circumstances allowed it, foreign imperialism at the mouths of the Danube, which sowed discord and provoked restlessness, trouble, and conflicts.

Thus, in the fourteenth century, right from their foundation, the voivodeships were compelled to fight against the claims of sovereignty on part of Hungarian and Polish kings — who disputed, in turn, the right of domination over these regions — as well as fight with them or often alone against Tartar domination coming from beyond the Dniester, and afterward against the Turkish expansion from beyond the Danube. Weakened by this continuous fight on all fronts, by dynastic rivalries fostered by those short-sighted neighbors, and on the other hand, abandoned by the Christians, the voivodeships were

Stephen the Great

compelled to accept Turkish sovereignty, resuming the fight later on as defenders of Christian civilization at the Danube under Stephen the Great, in the second half of the fifteenth century.

Attacked again from behind by their Christian neighbors who were much too selfish to realize the general importance of the mission that the voivodeships were fulfilling at the price of so many sacrifices, they had to bow again to the powerful Turkish Crescent until the end of the sixteenth century when they were to live through that short tragic epic, marked by the 8-year reign of Michael the Brave (1593-1601). Rising against the Ottoman Empire and succeeding in shaking off the Turkish yoke by his victories at Călugăreni and Giurgiu, and looked to as a liberator by the Christian populations in the Balkans, Michael was compelled to direct his troops towards Transylvania, because Prince Andrew Báthory, a typical example of Hungarian aristocratic egoism, wished to bring about his fall.

Moreover, the Voivodes of Wallachia possessed in Transylvania, even since 1366, several fiefs, namely: a) The Duchy of Făgăraș, comprising most of the actual district with the same name without the villages North of the Olt, but including the Northeastern part of the actual district of Târnava Mare; b) The Amlaș, with the eight villages West of Sibiu, including Săliștea, granted at the same date to Vladislav, the Voivode of Wallachia. Those regions remained under the Wallachian Voivodes' domination until 1478, that is to say for more than a hundred years.

On the other hand, Stephen the Great obtained from Matthias Corvinus two fortresses, Ciceiul (East of Dej) and Cetatea de Baltă (towards 1476). These fortresses were surrounded by 60 dependent villages (most of them Romanian), which means nearly all the county of Solnoc Dobâca of later on, and a part of the country of Cojocna (the actual district of Cluj). At Vad, one of those villages, Stephen the Great founded an Orthodox Bishophric for the Romanians of that region. In 1529, John Zápolya ceded to Petru Rareş, voivode of Moldavia, 50 villages around Bistriţa — with Rodna and the mining region — as well as Unguraşul, with 24 villages. A part of that extensive domain was lost in 1538, but Rodna, Unguraşul, and Ciceiul remained under Moldavian domination until 1561.

In the same situation were the fiefs of Vinţul-de-Jos and Vurpărul, near Sibiu, ceded to the Voivodes of Wallachia by the Voivode of Transylvania and taken back again by him several times during the first half of the sixteenth century.

After conquering Transylvania, Michael the Brave was compelled to occupy Moldavia too because the imperialistic egoism of another Christian state joined the Turks and menaced him from behind. Achieving thus for a short time, after so many centuries, the natural territorial unity of the Carpathian region within the framework of the state organization prevailing at that time, Michael the Brave was overthrown by the plotting of the aristocratic classes in Transylvania and by the ambitions of the Imperial general Basta. In face of the anarchy that spread immediately afterward, leaving the way open to foreign troops representing all the imperialisms of that epoch, from the Northeast, South, and Northwest, the Emperor in Vienna, faced with the danger of losing all possibility of realizing his claims and being dragged into unforeseen conflicts which this chaos might bring about, was compelled to entrust to the Romanian Voivode, in conjunction with general Basta, the task of reestablishing the old state of things and of putting matters in order again.

Only the Romanian Voivode had the possibility of reconquering Transylvania, but his rule depended on his excluding all foreign influences which sowed anarchy also in the neighboring voivodeships, namely Moldavia and Wallachia.

Michael's task however was brought to a premature and tragic end by the cowardly assassination of the Voivode at the very moment when he was about to proceed to Wallachia — after having conquered Transylvania — to complete the work that he had begun in such a promising way.

The bloody and thoughtless deed which stopped the reorganization of the political unity of the territories at the mouths of the Danube, by uniting all parts which had been artificially separated from one another, soon showed its fatal consequences.

The three countries fell again immediately under Turkish sovereignty, the Poles were driven from Moldavia, and the imperialists were turned out of Transylvania which was now in a complete state of anarchy.

All endeavors to revive, at least partially, in one form or another, the lost unity that now proved to be necessary for the suppressing of anarchy and the safeguarding of common interests, failed. Not even the alliance of Braşov with the Voivodes Radu Şerban and Radu Mihnea, Michael the Brave's successors on the throne, could restrain the predatory instincts of Gabriel Báthory, the Prince of Transylvania, who, embodying more conspicuously in his grotesque personality the ruthless tendencies of the ruling aristocratic classes in Transylvania,

Michael the Brave

demonstrated the fatal part they played in the country, and the unconscious help they gave by their mere existence to the decomposing factors coming from outside.

The defeat suffered is all the more significant because Braşov, due to its geographical position, almost in the territorial center of those three countries, and to its close connections for centuries past with both Moldavia and Wallachia on which her welfare, peace, and even her existence depended, was predestined from the very beginning to represent their common needs.

The failure of those efforts proved that without the murdered prince, without his leadership and more especially without the ethnic Romanian forces which Michael embodied, a re-establishment of the natural order — the expression of the common interest and the autochthonous conditions of lite — was utterly impossible.

Looked at in this light, Michael the Brave's short reign reveals in the dramatic vicissitudes of his stormy life, the factors which constantly hampered the evolution towards normalization and consolidation of law and order in Transylvania, and consequently in the whole Carpathian area and also those which were able to give those regions stability and the proper balance. The security and stability of the political situation at the mouths of the Danube were dependent on the state of affairs in Transylvania, which was the geographical center and the point of vantage of the whole country. Without Transylvania, it was natural that all the efforts of the two Voivodeships, Wallachia and Moldavia, should have remained fruitless, that their fall should have become inevitable and as a consequence, the field should have been left open for the unrestrained breaking out of all imperialisms which through colliding at this crossroad were fatally bound to extend the conflicts to other countries as well.

So that Michael the Brave's wish to acquire lasting sovereignty over the mouths of the Danube by uniting Transylvania, Moldavia, and Wallachia into a powerful and respected state organization, instinctively fulfilled one of the most deeply rooted tendencies of the entire region towards a political unity of its own and corresponded in its final aims to the general interest of having a more consolidated order and a more stable balance in the Danubian basin.

XV

The Romanian People and the Hungarian State in Face of the Unity of the Carpathian Regions; Ioan Corvin

That inborn inclination of the Romanian people to serve the tendencies of unification of the Carpathian provinces in autonomous forms of state was due to its autochthonic character and to its complete identification with the natural laws of the regions in which it lived.

A thousand-year-old familiarity with the surroundings gave it the possibility to adapt itself to the point of absorbing also many of the foreign elements brought there by circumstances and made it capable of expressing them instinctively in valid forms of an original mode of life.

That instinct of autochthony that characterizes the work of its great leaders as also the determining authorities of state life were so deeply rooted, that it even influenced the life of personalities who no longer belonged to the Romanian people by anything but blood.

Among these, the figure of Ioan Corvin of Hunedoara (John Hunyadi) stands out as a noble example.

A pure Romanian by origin, from the district of Hunedoara in the Southwest of Transylvania, the son of Voicu, one of those defenders of the border, ennobled by the King of Hungary for their deeds of military valor, Ioan Corvin cut himself off from his people by entering the class of Hungarian Catholic nobles.

His son Matthias, identifying himself with the superimposed forms of state organization, was to become the greatest and most brilliant King of Hungary, the promoter and protector of the cultural Renaissance of that country.

Ioan Corvin however remains, by his victories over the Turks, one the greatest heroes of Christendom, whose legendary fame has been sung in the popular poems of various nations.

For it was his bravery which kept for Christianity the boundary of the Danube in an age when brilliant Byzantium, "the Queen of cities", ended her glorious existence under the heel of the undefeatable Mehmed the Second.

Ioan Corvin ascended all the steps in the hierarchy of the medieval Hungarian state: as Ban of Severin he built the citadel of Timişoara to serve as a strategical center of the defensive system against the Turks; as Voivode of Transylvania and Count of the Szeklers, as Regent and Supreme Commander of Hungary he became the most prominent personality in the state during that period.

Nevertheless, going beyond the fixed horizon of the foreign world in which he had enrolled himself and beyond his official attributions, he — in answer probably to the secret call of the blood which ran through his veins — tried even as Stephen the Great and Michael the Brave, the great Romanian princes of later on, to give the whole of the Carpathian bastion the possibility of a unitary action of its own, by imposing a closer connection between the three countries of Transylvania, Wallachia, and Moldavia, so that together might constitute a more stable force

JOHAN HUNNIAD Gouverneur
van Hongarien etc.

at the mouths of the Danube; with the result that despite all the merits he had won for himself, Ioan Corvin was nevertheless compelled to endure the enmity of those same factors which, one and a half centuries later, brought about by their machinations the fall of Michael the Brave in Transylvania.

Actuated by the law of destiny, the aristocratic classes of the Hungarian Apostolic Kingdom also forced Ioan Corvin — because his personality had surpassed them and his constructive plans, based on autochthonous relations, clashed with the historical mission which the very artificialness of the state that created it had given it — to give up the dignities he had. And it was only at a moment of supreme and imminent peril for the whole Christian World, that the nobles allowed him to take up his leadership again and to die victorious while defending the citadel of Belgrade.

Thus twice, at two historical crossroads, are defined the trends and aims which the two determining factors through their constant antagonism had in the intensely dramatic development of the Carpathian geographical unity.

On one hand the Romanian people as an expression of autochthonous facts, on the other the privileged classes ruling over Transylvania, annihilating every attempt to consolidate the situation by their dogged opposition both against the regrouping of the countries in the natural geographical unity of the region and against the natural internal evolution towards a system of greater social equity and wider ethnic and political rights. For each of those factors was subject to the inherent laws of the causes which had created it.

The Romanian people followed the normal path of development following the historical fate which had placed it from ancient times in those parts. The superimposed aristocratic classes followed theirs, which depended on the conditions which had introduced them in the districts on the left of the Tisa as far as the Carpathians.

We have seen the factors and historical circumstances of the period when the Hungarian state was constituted in the form given to it by its founder, Stephen the Holy, the first apostolic King, under whom began the real domination of that state in Transylvania. We have also seen how the very life and territorial area of his creation were dependent on the aristocratic structure and on the Catholic missionary character of the state, embodied in the constitutional theory of "The Holy Crown"; as well as the gradual transformation of that organism of the state into a federation of privileged classes freeing itself more and more from the central authority of the Crown.

We shall now examine the consequences developed over the time, which the aristocratic structure and missionary character of the state had on the Romanian provinces on the left of the Tisa, which had been successively included in the medieval Hungarian Kingdom.

XVI

Penetration of Hungarian Domination into the Romanian Districts near the Tisa and in Transylvania

The Romanian people fast came to grips with the Hungarians a long time back, at the time when the Hungarians came to settle in Pannonia. According to the oldest historical source, an anonymous chronicler, appreciated anew by Hungarian science which praises today his work as being "one of the most harmonious creations of Latin medieval historiography", showing "methodical thought and deep knowledge just in those parts which refer to the coming of the Hungarians to Pannonia, the generals of Arpad fought victorious battles with various Romanian-Slavic voivodeships in the regions left of the Tisa, in Bihor, Transylvania, and Banat. These undoubtedly refer to certain incursions which the Hungarian tribes undertook, on their own, in those places as they had often in others.

The consequence of those actions could only be, at best, superficial nominal domination of the kind which other invading peoples had before them, without changing too much the forms of the collective life of the inhabitants.

But it was not until the new state organization of King Stephen I began a penetration action, that lasting consequences were left and trouble began. Due to this, penetration was much more difficult and encountered with serious resistance lasting two centuries, from the beginning of the eleventh to the beginning of the thirteenth century.

The foundation of the domination to come however was laid in the time of Stephen I, by the subjugation of the Northeastern regions in the valley of Someş, which were the widest means of penetration into Transylvania from the West.

At the end of the century, during the reign of Ladislas I, they were able to force the other Western road of penetration into Transylvania, subjugating the valleys of the Mureş and Târnava Mică. As an outward symbol of the new domination the Catholic episcopate at Alba Iulia, in Transylvania, was founded.

During the twelfth century, the regions in the center of Transylvania and the valley of the Olt were subdued, and early in the thirteenth century, the Ţara Bârsei was roped in by conferring it on the Order of the Teuton Cavaliers.

XVII

Character and Aims of Hungarian Domination
in those Regions

The new rulers intended to organize the conquered territory on the left of the Tisa after the manner of Pannonian Hungary, that is to say, to impose the existing Romanian "Cnezate" and "voivodeships" the territorial unities of the royal counties.

These forms of organization produced deep changes. The old leaders of the native population, the "cneji" and "voivodes", became village justice and assistants of the royal dignitaries. From that fallen state, however, they could, if they turned Catholic, rise and build up an advantageous economic position for themselves by appropriating the best parts of landed property, indivisible until then.

For, with the enthronement of the new rules, the native population fell into dependence, all the land being considered by the law as being royal property merely left in the possession of the ancient owners. Thus, the gradual detaching of the native leaders from their national community was prepared by their ennoblement and the bestowal of estates on them. For royal donations ennobled and conferred on the recipient full rights and powers over the land received.

In the bestowal of these favors, preference was given to bodies of the Catholic Church. Besides, owing to the fewness of the new rulers, several foreigners were called in to help, whose regions being handed over to them for autonomous government, the "quality of guests", attributed to foreigners giving their collective organization the possibility of benefitting from the nobiliary rights of property in the way that the other noble recipients of donations did individually.

The Saxons who settles in compact groups in the Center and Southwest of Transylvania were colonists of that type, who had come from Germany in the second half of the twelfth century and the beginning of the thirteenth, attracted by the privileged situation offered to them. The Szeklers were probably remnants of a Mongolian refuge population colonized, with special border privileges, along the Eastern boundaries of the country.

All these measures however could not make up for the lack in a number of the new rules. Due to this, the old popular organizations of the native populations continued to exist in many places for a long while after, and the wounds caused to the ethnic block of the Romanian native population did not prove mortal.

For, as has been seen, the Hungarian penetration into the regions left of the Tisa had the character of complete dispossession and on the ruins of what had been, the new order was raised, which by its structure depended on the kind of land ownership: all those who owned no titled properties conferred by the king in some form or other, did not belong to the privileged classes and by that very fact no longer formed part of the community of the state.

In the few documents which still exist on the epoch previous to the great Tartar invasion of 1241, which devastated and destroyed "all the regions as far as the Tisa" when any mention is made of Romanians, it usually refers to the taking away of a part of their common property in order to confer it by royal donation on members of one of the three categories of privileged classes.

For already then the form of government was being prepared that evolution was to give to the provinces left of the Tisa, within the medieval Hungarian state, by a union of the 3 different privileged classes, constituted based on the 3 categories of privileged rights in 3 distinct territorial circumscriptions: the nobles and ecclesiastical organizations in the North, Center, and West, the Saxons in the South Center and North-East and between them on the North-Eastern border of Transylvania, the Szeklers.

The weak connections with the medieval Hungarian Kingdom, owing to the eccentric geographical situation of those regions, prevented their complete fusion with the rest of the country, causing even the new superimposed forms of the State organization created by royal grace, to work differently in a political particularism suited to the natural conditions of the country, often even in flagrant opposition to the far-away central authority.

That natural particularism compelled recognition from the Crown itself, forcing it under the influence of the autochthonous political creations of before the conquest, to give the government of these regions to a special dignitary called Voivode. And the Voivodes of Transylvania, although they were royal dignitaries and often even sons of the sovereign, exercised their attributions on a territory which stretched even to the Tisa, "in directions often hostile to be able to rule it according to their will, giving estates to those they trusted and taking no notice of the autonomies established in royal privileges.

The privileged classes of that region developed in a like manner, making use of a general movement towards an ever-growing autonomy of the feudal factors, which was started in the whole Hungarian Kingdom after the Tartar invasion, when the kings were forced by numerous and large donations from their own domains, to reduce the very basis of their power to secure the help of all instruments of State for the reconstruction of the country.

In 1291 the privileged classes of these regions succeeded in obtaining for the first time the convocation of a Transylvanian Diet, in which Romanians also took part beside the Nobles, Szeklers, and Saxons, with the object of discussing the improvement of existing conditions.

Owing to the ruins left by the Tartar invasion, the privileged classes, in order to be able to put things straight again, were also compelled to accept help from any side and to recognize the old popular organizations of the Romanians.

For, under the fragile construction of the privileged State, the ethnical reality of the native population continued to exist and was so great, that it was able to assimilate — overcoming all obstacles which the privileged order put in its way — even the Hungarians and the Saxons, thus threatening the apostolic character of the Kingdom. This caused Pope Gregory IX, in 1234, to make a protest to the junior king, the future Bela IV, "in the interest of those Hungarians and Germans in the Kingdom of Hungary who, having become one people with the Wallachians, ignored the German Catholic bishop of Cumania, receiving the sacraments from some pseudo-bishops who practiced Grecian rites."

Hence it was quite natural that the attempts of the Hungarian Kingdom to extend its rule by superimposing that same privileged order also South of the Carpathians should fail, for here the Romanian "voivodeships" and "cnezates" had, through their union under the nominal domination of the neighboring barbarian peoples — of the Pechenegs, the Cumans and the Tartars — become sufficiently strong to resist successfully attempts of that kind and to build on natural ethnical foundations a State life of their own, whose role in the defense of the Danube frontier manifested itself in the history of Moldavia and Wallachia during the centuries which followed, in the manner already shown.

But in the medieval Hungarian Kingdom, the unstable fragile ethnical foundation forced the kings, in order to give the privileged State organization more vigor, to cede whole territories in the interior of the country to a Mongolian kindred population, such for instance the Cumans, and also to abandon large estates to the hands of just a few who, succeeding in raising themselves above their privileged fellows, constituted themselves into a special class of magnates.

Against those all-powerful magnates, all the other nobles, whose privileges the king could now no longer protect, organized themselves, usurping and appropriating rights and incomes which until then they had had through the king's goodwill. Thus there came into being the "comitatus nobiliares" (counties), similar to a federation of groups of privileged bodies set over the different regions and monopolizing for the assemblies of those local oligarchs, the so-called country meetings, all the attributions of the State.

That development definitively divided the population of the country into two different categories hostile to one another, on the one hand, the privileged classes of all categories forming the State, and on the other hand, the oppressed working population which had no rights of state and which now depended entirely on the goodwill of local masters, having lost its situation as vassals of the king with the privileged classes as intermediaries, and having become the direct and exclusive serfs, in the proper sense of that word, of the local masters who owned the land.

The Angevin dynasty, enthroned in Hungary after the extinction of the Arpads with the effective help of the Pope and which came from the international knighthood milieu produced by the Crusades, had neither the intention nor the capacity, nor as a matter of fact, the power, to redress that situation. On the contrary, it sharpened the Catholic religious character of the State so that the situation of the Romanians belonging to the Orthodox Church became even more difficult.

An immediate consequence of those changed situations was the rebellion of the Voivode Bogdan of Maramureş, who, forced to leave his native country, founded with his followers the independent Voivodeship of Moldavia.

The Angevin kings, although they did not conceive the State on national foundations, only as a confederation of privileged classes and fighters, nevertheless turned on religious grounds against the great mass of their Romanian subjects. For the latter's forms of the traditional organization, they could have no sympathy; at most they could admit the existence of those Romanian princedoms near the boundary of the Danube, as a means of defense against the Turks. From among these sprang later on the well-known figure of Ioan Corvin.

But to this, the growingly insecure state of affairs within the country corresponded an adventurous tendency to expand without, due to and favored by the dynastic claims of the kings. For that reason the medieval Hungarian Kingdom made offensive wars against almost all its neighbors, from Naples and Venice to Lithuania and Poland, from Bohemia and Austria unto Moldavia, Wallachia, and the Balkan Peninsula, weakening by that anarchical dynasty imperialism, inherent in the non-national character of the State, the power of resistance of the countries in the path of the Ottoman Empire, and so helping unconsciously the menacing advance of the Turks against Christianity, and even prepared without wanting to, the later fall of its own country at the battle of Mohács (1526).

So that far from fulfilling the historical mission for which the Apostolic Kingdom had been created, namely to form in the Danubian basin a bastion of Christian civilization against invasions, the medieval Hungarian State proved only an element of unrest which, disorganizing Central Europe by its extreme imperialism and by its internal weakness, caused by the violation of real conditions and existing ethnical facts through a constitutional order and social hierarchy flagrantly unsuitable and contradictory to the natural conditions, even opened the way at a moment of great trial for the whole Western civilization, to those invasions towards the heart of Europe.

The unstableness of the Hungarian Kingdom of the Middle Ages grew during the last century before its fall, both owing to the constant fights and struggles for the occupation of the throne and more especially through the institution of mercenary armies which, freeing the privileged classes who ruled the country from their last obligation to the community, turned them towards that narrow and ferocious egoism, concentrated in the desire to ensure for themselves as many benefits as possible, and to exploit to the utmost the population subjected to them and completely at their mercy.

Consequently, it is not surprising that conditions being such, the Hungarian Kingdom of the Middle Ages, despite its great territorial area, should fall before the Ottoman attack, while much smaller states and far more exposed, such as Moldavia and Wallachia, were successful in keeping the aggressor at bay and even in preserving their own character.

XVIII

The Genesis of the Transylvanian Autonomous
Principality; "Unio Trium Nationum"; Dozsa's
Rebellion, the Tripartite Code of Law,
and the Mohács Disaster

Indeed the mentality of the privileged classes had reached a
point that made impossible the maintenance of any collective
organization.

Two contemporary witnesses have characterized in drastic
and conclusive terms the mentality of the privileged classes.
Massaro, one of them, describing the leaders of the country at
that time, affirms «that there was no injustice or shameful action
they would not do for money»; and the other, Burgio, that "if
Hungary could be saved from the engulfing Turkish peril for the
payment of three florins, one could not find three men in the
whole country ready to make that sacrifice."

More eloquent however than any testimonies are the events
which preceded the Mohács catastrophe.

The dissolution of the State began in Transylvania in the year
1437, when religious persecutions started there again during the
reign of Sigismund of Luxemburg. George Lepes, Bishop of
Transylvania, tried to impose the tithe for the Catholic religion
on populations of other creeds. The peasants, composed of

Romanians, and of some Szeklers and Hungarians who had been treated unfairly, rebelled and took up their stand in a fortified camp on Mount Bobâlna, in order to obtain satisfaction for their grievances.

The army of the nobles led by the Voivode of Transylvania having been defeated, he was obliged to begin peace negotiations and to sign on 7 June 1437, the treaty of Cluj-Mănăştur, by which the privileged classes renounced the giving of patrimonial sentences, to the royalties which had been concessioned to them in 1351, and to most of the forced labor and service which the vassals were compelled to render to their feudal lord. Following that arrangement, the peasants were to be considered as a distinct class, with the right to choose as upholders of their own interests certain leaders whose person would be considered inviolable.

As the carrying out that contract was equivalent to a complete abolishment of the existing conditions, the privileged classes, that is to say, the nobles, the Saxons' deputies, and the Szeklers' representatives, met under the presidency of the Vice-Voivode of Transylvania in September of that same year at Căpâlna, and formed an alliance by which they obliged themselves to give each other help against any adversary and to make common protests to the king, in the event of the latter committing any injustices towards anyone of the three "nations."

That was the very first time that the privileged classes in Transylvania arrogated to themselves the title of "nations." The term must be understood in the limited sense of the privileged constitution and not in the ethical sense, prevalent in the world today.

One of the most deliberate and most persistently repeated confusions made use of by Hungarian science and historiography, in order to give a false perspective to the situation in Transylvania, is the national meaning attributed to that idea which was totally foreign to it. As the term will keep on recurring because it indicates a phenomenon that constitutes the very foundation of Transylvania's historical State organization, the exact understanding of its meaning is absolutely necessary.

That alliance, a real separatist confederacy, was entitled "Unio Trium Nationum" and embodied the old particularist tendencies of the privileged classes in Transylvania; it also showed their intention to monopolize completely for themselves, even in opposition to the legitimate sovereign, the ruling of the country, as well as their determination to maintain unimpaired all the exceptional advantages which a privileged situation had given them. Royal authority was thus weakened still more, and the majority of the inhabitants still more cruelly oppressed.

But without the armed help of the privileged classes in Pannonian Hungary, the "Union" would not have been able to make any headway, for its own armies while they fought alone were defeated by those of the native population. After victory had been achieved with foreign help, terrible persecutions begun against the peasants who from that time onward were really tied to the land.

It was only the complete abdication of the King from the functions and attributions of arbiter which were incumbent on him, that made possible the outbreak of that real civil war, with such fatal consequences for the future both concerning the King's authority and to the existence of the State.

"The Union of the three nations" was formed with a well-defined aim in view, the seizing of power and the exclusive government in the country, and not as has often been affirmed, as a means of defense against the outside peril represented by the Turks. The proof is that the renewal of that union was made with the same aim in view in 1459 at Mediaş, namely to defend "the liberties" of the privileged classes if necessary with arms, against King Matthias Corvinus, who wished to re-establish his authority, repressing any arbitrary action committed by the privileged class. Matthias Corvinus even intended to consolidate the organism of the State by a fairer distribution of taxes, abolishing the exemption of the nobles and clergy by the introduction of a general land tax.

The rebellion in 1467 of the three privileged classes in Transylvania united by that treaty of mutual assistance, quickly suppressed, showed the boldness of their intentions, which even then aimed at complete emancipation from the king's authority, even at the price of the dismembering of the State.

With that occasion, other terms appeared, which were to dominate the public life of Transylvania in the centuries to come and were to form a new opportunity for confusion, through attributing to them meanings different from those that were really theirs.

To seize the whole power of the State in their selfish class interest, the Transylvanian privileged classes used and were to use the high-sounding formula "of the fight against oppression to maintain liberties", meaning by "liberty" the unhindered possibility of abuses and by "oppression" any attempt to reestablish order in the State organization.

The alleged liberty aimed at by the "Union of the three nations" showed itself in Transylvania on the one hand in the cruel oppression of the dependent population of the Romanian peasants, and on the other, in acts of treason to King and country. Their horrible and inhuman cruelty to the peasants showed itself on the occasion of Dozsa's rebellion, and the acts of treason provoked the disaster of Mohács and the fall of the Hungarian Apostolic Kingdom. Those two events are significant, affecting all subsequent development.

The peasant revolt under Dozsa had its birth in a Crusade movement. Giovani Medici, the son of Lorenzo the Magnificent having been elected Pope in 1513 under the name Leon X, in order to appease him conferred on Thomas Bakocz, Archbishop of Hungary, who had wanted the Pontifical Crown for himself, the dignity of Apostolic Legate for the whole South-East of Europe and wide powers to enable him to organize a crusade against the Turks. The Papal bull published at Easter of that same year, by promising crusaders, besides forgiveness of all sins, liberation from serfdom and full freedom of person and property for themselves and their families left at home, created an unheard of sensation and attracted into the crusaders' camps innumerable peasants, longing to escape from the oppression of their masters.

Because the nobility sabotaged the action, the Papal Legate entrusted the command of the masses to George Dozsa, a man of the people, who had distinguished himself in the fights against the Turks.

The privileged classes frightened by the largeness of the movement began to catch and to punish cruelly the peasants who ran away to enlist themselves, causing thus an unheard of agitation in the crusaders" camps. As a result, numerous groups headed by Dozsa began reprisal expeditions.

The army of the nobles under Stephen Báthory, the "comes" of Timişoara, having defeated a part of the crusaders, committed so many atrocities, mutilating the vanquished and sending them home in a maimed state, that it provoked a general revolt of the peasants. Armies of rebels sprang up on all sides; one formed of Romanians was defeated at Oradea Mare; many were forced to flee to Maramureş and to emigrate from there into Moldavia and Poland. Dozsa, who with the principal army had succeeded in the end in crushing the army of the nobles, conceived the plan of reforming the State radically by a division of lands and the abolishment of the privileged classes set over them.

In the meantime, the army of the three privileged classes, led by John Zápolya, Voivode of Transylvania, having succeeded after bloody fights in repressing the movement in their own country, turned at the request of Stephen Verböczy against Dozsa and destroyed the principal army outside Timişoara.

The orgy of revenge that followed surpassed anything imaginable, revealing the whole unlashed fury of those who had seen for a moment their privileged rule imperiled. The crusaders were tracked everywhere and having been brought home were tortured, mutilated, and branded with red hot irons. Dozsa "the King of the Kurutz", as he was jeeringly nicknamed, after 40 days of imprisonment and starvation, was set on a red hot iron throne with a red hot iron crown on his brow and his comrades were compelled to swallow the flesh tom off with red hot tongs from the body of their chief who was being roasted alive.

The horror of contemporaries inured though they were to the many deeds of cruelties customary in that age of transition at the beginning of the sixteenth century, was so great at the sight of that terrible spectacle, that it gave birth to the legend that Voivode Zápolya went suddenly blind before the altar while mass was being celebrated and that only after his mother and sister had prayed fervently for two whole years was the Heaven-sent punishment removed.

The privileged classes however looked upon him as their savior and at their country meetings discussed raising him to the throne. At the same time, they did without loss of time everything possible to give a definite character to the exceptional situation which they had won through their bloody deeds.

For that purpose, considering that the punishment of the rebellious population should be extended also to their descendants so that any attempt to overturn their domination should not be repeated, the Diet brought in a law which tied the peasants definitively to the land as perpetual serfs of their feudal lord. And in order to make their class domination still more secure, it forbade the peasants under dire penalties to carry arms. If for instance a peasant were caught with a rifle in his hands, his right hand would be cut off.

Dissatisfied, in their unrestrained lust for vengeance and boundless desire to dominate, with mere decisions of the Diet, the privileged classes, in order to give a still greater guarantee of stableness to the privileged classes, adopted a complete code of laws, the famous "Opus tripartitum" compiled by the protonotary Stephen Verböczy, a relative of the Voivode Zápolya and his adviser during the rebellion.

Verböczy's code, which has its place among the bloodiest and most cruel collections of laws of antiquity, defined in a multitude of paragraphs the consuetudinary law in the interpretation given it by the privileged classes, under the influence of their lust for revenge.

In it is exposed — on the very eve of the country's fall — the constitutional theory of the "Holy Crown", in it being established that "the freedom of the nobility constituted the essence of State", while the unprivileged mass of the population not forming part of State, remained "the wretched and paying plebs" condemned to "mera et perpetua servitude."

XIX
Character of the Transylvanian Principality

The "Opus tripartitum" was the juridical guide and the constitutional basis of Transylvania in the period which followed. The principles of political and social injustice which it laid down corresponded so closely to the desires and mentality of the ruling classes, that foreigners nicknamed the Hungarian privileged nobility "Populus Verböczyanus", and the nobles asked as recently as the middle of the eighteenth century, on the eve of the Great French Revolution, their then sovereign, a Habsburg, to restore without any modification the liberties and constitution as fixed by the tripartite code.

Stephen Verböczy, its author, as a reward, was elected Palatine of the Kingdom, acquiring thus the power to govern the country in the spirit of his laws and to lead it to disaster. And as a crowning of the destructive role they played, the privileged classes of Transylvania — the "three nations" — under the leadership of their highly lauded Voivode John Zápolya, committed, at the moment of the greatest trial, also an act of treason against their country, by not taking part with their army in the unfortunate battle which took place on 29 August 1526 on the marshy places South of Mohács.

By the annihilation of the army and the death of its last king, Louis II, medieval Hungary really ceased to exist, the way being now left open to the Turks right up to the heart of Europe, namely right up to Vienna.

The events which followed the occupation of Hungary, the siege of Vienna, the fight for the crown between Ferdinand of Austria and John Zápolya until the establishment of the Turkish pashalik in Hungary, were nothing but the gradual liquidation of the old State organization of the Apostolic Kingdom following the interests and aims of the Sultan Suleiman, the unopposed arbiter of the situation. The nobles themselves, though they were the established and representative instruments of the old privileged State, had recourse to the arbitrage of the Sultan, to maintain for themselves an influential position in the new political order about to be formed in the wake of the disaster which they themselves had provoked.

John Zápolya and Ferdinand of Austria, the two competitors who had been elected kings illegally in separate diets, each by a party of the nobles, addressed themselves to the Sultan for the recognition of their title. John Zápolya more especially, who was the favorite representative of the privileged classes, considering himself to be the candidate of a party which dared to call itself "national", acted with the same total lack of scruples and respect for the interests of the community which had characterized his behavior during the fight at Mohács.

Through Jeronim Lasczky, the envoy he sent to Constantinople, he did not hesitate to offer himself and the country he desired to the Sultan, assuring him that he would be his friend and the enemy of all his adversaries and undertaking to pay a tribute of money and to guarantee by hostages his complete submission to the Sultan, his Suzerain-Lord, and the free passing through his country of Turkish troops.

The Turks however, as they told General Habordansky,
Ferdinand's envoy, considered Hungary as belonging to them:
"Wherever the hoof of the Sultan's horse has trodden we rule;
we have destroyed the king of Hungary, and his Kingdom is
henceforth in our hands and we can keep it or give it to
whomsoever we please. Your master can only become king of
Hungary on the day on which we shall crown him."

For his shameless and faithless behavior, Zápolya was
excommunicated by a Papal bull. Despite all the humiliating and
treasonable actions committed, the total liquidation of the
Hungarian State, prepared and caused by the interested and
selfish attitude of the ruling classes which had represented it,
was not long in coming. In 1540 Suleiman again occupied Buda
and extending Turkish domination to the center of Europe,
transformed the Pannonian plain into a Turkish pashalik. This
was followed at a short interval by the occupation of the Banat
through the conquest in 1551 of Timişoara, a citadel built one
century earlier by Ioan Corvin to form a bastion against the
Turkish peril.

The appointment of Verböczy as the supreme judge of the
Christians in Buda, within the Turkish rule, is significant for the
role which the privileged classes, led by John Zápolya, played in
that tragedy, and the Peace of Adrianople in 1568 confirmed by
a public document of international law the liquidation of the
medieval Hungarian State, recognizing the absolute domination
of the Porte in central Hungary as well as the sovereignty of the
Sultan on all territories which had belonged to that state, both
Christian competitors to the Crown, namely Emperor
Maximilian II, the successor of his Father Ferdinand I and John
Sigismund Zápolya, Prince of Transylvania, son of the Voivode

John Zápolya of a sad memory, having to pay tribute to the Porte for the territories which they still retained from the dividing up of the "Apostolic Kingdom."

The catastrophic disappearance of the Hungarian Kingdom of the Middle Ages proved the impossibility of uniting the distinct regions of the Danubian basin into a privileged form of state, for, contrary to the aims of the ruling factors which at a historic moment favored and upheld it, it was not possible to obtain the stableness and the wished-for balance in these parts, which were necessary to the development of European civilization.

On the contrary, instead of constituting a positive element in the grand work of reconstruction of the Middle Ages, the Hungarian State proved to be, during the whole course of its existence, a weakening factor of the whole political system and a permanent threat to its neighbors and in general to the security of the whole Western World.

The. ever-growing internal unstableness and the more and more disproportionate external imperialism of the Apostolic Kingdom expressed the total inability of the Hungarian people to adapt itself to the new conditions of life of a State, which had not been created from its own national resources but through the strong will of one man and which, in consequence, did not correspond to its real needs but on the contrary exceeded by far and weakened its ethnical possibilities. Owing to this, the feudal system of the Hungarian Kingdom being from the very beginning too artificial in character did not fulfill the necessary role of an element of transition towards the all-embracing forms of the national State but retained exclusively the character of a governing instrument, set over varying regions and foreign peoples incapable of expressing the real deeply rooted interest of the surrounding milieu. Lacking therefore entirely that instinctive discipline which only the feeling of ethnic solidarity can give, the privileged classes of the Hungarian Kingdom of the Middle Ages could not but remain the totally enslaved prisoners of an instinct to dominate which had no other general purpose beyond that.

Dominated exclusively by that instinct, the only real thing about them, it was only natural that the privileged classes should permanently keep that attitude of narrow and brutal selfishness which brought about the internal destruction and the external collapse of the whole edifice of state.

Due to that all powerful instinct, these classes had even in the tragic moments of the country's fall the already stated attitude of criminal complicity and shameless submission towards the foreign conqueror, their only worry being to save and keep unimpaired the exceptional privileges which they had secured.

The weakening of the authority of the Head of the State suited their purposes admirably, for in the same proportion their authority and power grew.

That parallelism of interests made it very easy for the foreign conqueror and the particularist elements within the country to sign an agreement on the ruins of the old forms of state. By that agreement, the possibilities of domination without limits by the ruling classes were not only maintained but even increased. Under the protection of Turkish sovereignty, the privileged classes were able to realize their wishes completely, taking over as absolute masters for 150 years, the fragile state organization of the Transylvanian Principality.

So that far from disappearing with it, the factors of unrest and disorganization of the old State survived it with increased vigor and possibilities, hindering also in the future by their fanaticism of oppression every attempt to give the Danubian basin more peace and stableness through an order more suitable to the natural conditions of those parts.

Due to them, all projects which aimed at normalization of the situations in a superior and more general interest, either by the creation of a centralized administration and a fairer state of equality of the populations and nations in the setting of an absolutist and unitary state or by a federalization of the various regions based on national autonomy could not be realized, being continually opposed by those privileged classes who in their negative actions continually made use of the much exploited and constantly repeated formula "the constitutional liberties."

Those "constitutional liberties", invoked every time they were asked to renounce in the general interest to a part of their privileges, were, as a matter of fact, only exceptional liberties of oppression and abusive exploitation, in the manner in which the privileged classes of Transylvania had ensured them for one another, first by the famous "union of the three nations" and then permanently by the Verböczy's tripartite code of laws.

For the autonomous Principality of Transylvania during those 150 years of Turkish suzerainty was not a unitary organism of State, but only an alliance of oppression of those three privileged classes directed, nominally, by the phantom authority of the prince elected by their diets.

Wishing to put on record that the constitutional base of the Principality of Transylvania under Turkish suzerainty was the famous union of the three nations, they renewed it immediately after the constitution of the new State, in the year 1542, and kept on renewing it all through the historical existence of that State.

The ruler of the country, the Prince, was nothing but a mandatory confirmed by the Porte, who was charged with the limited agenda common to the "three nations." In the hierarchy of the Ottoman Empire, the Prince had his definite place, he was subordinate to the Great Vizier and the Caïmacam and stood on equal footing with the pashas of Buda, Timişoara, and Oradea. Both his internal and external policies were under the ostensible tutorship of the Porte. In his foreign policy, he was not entitled to begin any war without the previous consent of the Porte. By not respecting that obligation, George Rákoczi II was deposed in 1675.

In his internal policy, the Prince was obliged to keep on good terms with the three privileged classes and to respect and protect their customs and prerogatives.

The diets, that is to say, the common assemblies of the privileged classes, had even the exclusive right, of passing laws, their decisions being often executed without having been confirmed by the Prince. The Prince had not the right to do the very least thing without informing the Princely Council, which was the elected exponent of the diet. Without its consent he could not carry on any negotiations whatever, neither send nor receive deputations, nor even read the letters received from abroad, and of course, still less make donations or confer rights. For the Porte looked upon the Prince of Transylvania as being its deputy, entrusted merely with the administration of Transylvania and of the neighboring Hungarian districts, whom it had the right to depose at any minute and put a pasha in his stead. In 1634 it actually intended to affect that change and in 1658, 1659, and 1661 it plainly threatened to do so.

Hence the Turkish suzerainty was not just nominal but very effective indeed. It had however the character of an agreement made with the privileged classes, the Prince being nothing but an executive instrument subordinated to them.

Using that agreement the Turks rewarded their former allies who had opened the way for them to the heart of Europe; besides it was not in their interest to favor the internal consolidation of Transylvania which, once realized, might have turned against the Porte's interest also. The privileged classes on the other hand were very glad to know that their rule of oppression was ensured and guaranteed by the imposing authority and power of the Sultan.

Neither the humiliating situation nor the heavy taxes which the Turkish suzerainty imposed on the country moved them, for it was not they who had to bear them but the Romanians, that wretched and money paying pleb which had been given over to their domination, exploitation, and oppression.

Having obtained an "Athnamé" in 1566 by which the Sultan having fixed the legal situation of Transylvania, obliged himself to maintain and protect their "liberties", the privileged classes saw all their wishes and efforts fulfilled, the rest, namely the dismembering of the "Apostolic Kingdom", the anarchy and decomposition of the Danubian basin which had become a permanent amphitheater of war, the menace to Christian civilization did not interest them at all for — as a well-known Hungarian historian put it — by keeping the privileged form through which the nobility had a preponderant situation, "Transylvania was able to have a Hungarian policy", the policy of the holders of the land. And that "Hungarian policy" in Transylvania as well as in the Western parts of the former kingdom now under the rule of the Habsburgs was characterized by "the oppression of the weak by the strong, by preventing those who had been wronged from voicing their wrongs and by efforts to assimilate by force, other peoples."

The State consisted of an unstable union of three distinct territories submitted to the exclusive domination of one of the three privileged bodies, the Hungarian and Szekler aristocracies and the Saxon oligarchy, each of which had different interests and quite often a different foreign policy. They suspected one another, quarreled continually, and were only in agreement on one single question, namely the common oppression of the population and the unimpaired maintenance of their "liberties." If those "liberties" were in danger of being even slightly impaired, they fell into accord at once and acted in common as they had done during the short reign of Michael the Brave. Because that Prince had dared to interfere concerning their exemption from taxes and to impose a general tax of 6 florins per gate, they joined hands to overturn him and, even after his death, spoke and thought of him with vindictive hatred.

If however their desires or interests required it, the privileged classes abandoned their attitude of rigid conservativism and even accepted revolutionary innovations. Thus when different forms of reformed religions sprang up in their midst, they did not hesitate to declare the Lutheran, Calvinistic and Unitarian religions "accepted" and recognized as having the same rights and prerogatives as the Catholic religion, thus attacking the very foundation on which the whole privileged system had been built. Only the Orthodox religion of the Romanians in Transylvania continued to be excluded from that recognition, for it was not the religion of any of the three privileged bodies. On the contrary, the Orthodox religion of the Transylvanian Romanians underwent during that period of so-called tolerance the harshest and most humiliating persecutions and interdictions.

As in all the other domains of their activity, the privileged classes tried to break the natural unity of the Romanian Orthodox Church, based on the same ethical foundation in the three neighboring countries: Transylvania, Moldavia, and Wallachia. With that aim in view some of them, namely the Saxons, tried to make proselytes among the Romanians, printing and distributing Romanian translations from holy books interpreted in the Lutheran sense. Their activity, however, did not produce the desired effect, it produced in fact a contrary effect to the one expected, it brought about the birth of a literary language and of literature of the traditional religion which were the first manifestations of a national Romanian conscience.

Then the Hungarian princes and nobles of Calvinistic faith began to use violent means to prevent the natural uninterrupted connections which existed between the Orthodox Church of Transylvania and that of Wallachia. Thus the Romanian Church was passed forcibly under the jurisdiction of a Calvinistic superintendent and the priests who would not preach the new faith were threatened with heavy fines and expulsion, they being also forbidden to cross the frontier into Wallachia and to receive the priests ordained in that country, as was the traditional custom.

The priests were also made serfs attached to the land and subjected to all oppressions and abuses of the lords of the land.

During that period in the life of the autonomous principality, the oligarchy of the privileged classes gave full play to their rooted fanaticism of oppression, abolishing the few privileges which the "Apostolic Kings" had granted to the Romanians in some parts and establishing by law the Romanian people's position "as dependent on the good pleasure of the princes and citizens", that is to say of the members of the three privileged classes. "That people", so ran an article of law, "being only admitted into the country in the public interest", because it formed the productive part of the population, "it had nevertheless dared to ask to be exempted from work and service on holidays. It is strictly forbidden for it to lay any more such claims before the Hungarian nation" that is to say before the nobility. And to prevent any possibility of improving their situation "it was decided that neither the clergy of the Romanians could be ennobled or entitled to have estates." Without any reticence whatever, the principle was then decreed that the State was composed of the only three privileged "nations" and four "accepted" religions, the Orthodox religion and Romanian population not being part of the State. The latter was merely tolerated so that its work should produce the things necessary for the public good.

The exclusivist oligarchic regime of those "three nations", which transformed the situation of the population into "an unbearable slavery" and the rule of the privileged "into a tyranny without a sense of responsibility", culminated in that last and lapidary constitutional expression.

Baron Wesselényi, a great Hungarian patriot, named these 7 fundamental principles of the constitutional order, the "seven capital sins of Transylvania." And yet, even today, Hungarian historiography speaks of that epoch of the Transylvanian autonomous principality as the golden age. That age was golden only for the privileged Hungarian nobility who was able to realize all their desires. For the country however the golden age meant total anarchy inside and out, a splitting up into three separate territories, each owned exclusively by one of the three privileged bodies, unending intrigues, and rivalries between those three privileged bodies, the institution of the most cynical and abnormal political, social, economic, national and religious oppression, a humble and servile attitude towards the strong and indescribable brutality towards the weak.

And looking at it from a general point of view, that "golden age" meant complete anarchy in the Danubian basin, transformed into a permanent battlefield right in the middle of Europe.

The culminating moment of the "constitutional liberties" praised ceaselessly by the ruling classes united in the 3 privileged "nations" of Transylvania, shows itself to have been a state of complete disorganization of the Danubian basin, transformed into a volcano which was a permanent peril through its innumerable conflicts and surprises for the peace of Europe and Western civilization.

XX

The Passing of Transylvania under the Domination of the Habsburgs; Tendencies and Aims of that Domination

With the defeat of the Turks before Vienna in 1683, a new historical era began, characterized by the victorious offensive of the Christians, who not only had succeeded in reconquering the lost territories but even threatened the domination of the Porte in Europe. Thus was the "Eastern Question" born, which was only settled by the end of World War.

The Eastern question, dominated by the Russian-Austrian rivalry in competition for the inheritance of the Ottoman Empire, was to provoke in concordance with the spirit of the times the national emancipation of the Christian peoples of those parts and to give birth to a new system of international equilibrium, founded on the existence of the independent national states in the Danubian basin and Balkan Peninsula.

In face of the victorious imperial counteroffensive, which represented Western civilization in this part of the world, having occupied the Pannonian plain and reached the Tisa and the Danube, the Transylvanian principality of the privileged "three nations" was unable to continue in its anarchical form under the protection of the Turkish suzerainty, and was compelled to identify with the projects for the reorganization of the Danubian basin, submitting to the rule of the Emperor in Vienna. Exactly as had happened 150 years before, when the Hungarian "Apostolic Kingdom" had fallen, the privileged classes of Transylvania were again solely preoccupied, during that historical upheaval, with the safeguarding of the privileges of their caste by the maintenance of their "constitutional liberties."

For that reason, negotiations were immediately begun with the Imperial generals. They lost no time in ratifying the agreement signed, which guaranteed them, in exchange for the recognition of the Emperor's suzerainty and the payment of an annual tribute, the preservation of the old constitutional forms, and of the unstable government of the Prince, who was the docile and interested executor of their aims. The Emperor in Vienna however knew very well, from his own experience in the regions which he had inherited from the former Hungarian Kingdom, the anarchical mentality and real aims of those privileged classes, and was not inclined in the very least to satisfy them. On the contrary, he aimed at ensuring order and peace in the Danubian basin by the organization of an administration as centralized as possible, and by the institution of his absolute power in a Unitarian State, in which all particularist forces were to be reduced as much as possible, to make room for as complete a leveling of the population of the whole empire as possible.

In fact, the Emperor was obliged in his own interest to oppose and mistrust the privileged classes for, apart from the danger and hamper which their particularist tendency constituted for his authority, their rule had impoverished the population to such an extent, that it simply could not pay the fiscal dues necessary to support the State, and their abusive exploitation had caused emigrations in such large masses, that the requirements to complete the army could no longer be met.

As a first measure to strengthen his authority and to establish order in the country, the Emperor took the opportunity of the death of Michael Apafi I, the last prince of Transylvania, not to appoint anyone else in his place. Taking it in his own charge, he wished to emancipate the country's administration from the all-powerful privileged classes by the institution of a Governor and a Transylvanian aulic chancery in Vienna, that were to act as a connecting link between the Center and the far off province; while in Transylvania the authority of the commanding general, upheld by the effective power of the military garrisons, was to ensure for him the role of head commander to the extent that his simple advice should have the value of orders.

At the same time, considering that the spiritual authority of the Catholic Church would be the best support for his rule, he tried, even making use of violent compulsory means, to spread that faith as much as possible among his subjects. Having won them over by promising to improve their material and moral situation and ensuring their acceptance among the religions recognized by the Transylvanian constitution — which meant their inclusion among the privileged — he convinced a number of Romanian priests and archpriests from Transylvania to leave the Orthodox Church and to declare themselves united with Rome; they had the right to keep their own religious forms so long as they recognized the Pope's authority as supreme and accepted certain dogmatic standards.

The inherent resistance of the Romanian people against all attempts to change its faith, which it considered to be a new means of oppression and a new attempt to injure its ethnic nature, as well as the successful opposition in the name of "constitutional liberties" made by the privileged classes' representatives in the Diet to the fulfillment of any promises made by the Emperor, practically killed his attempt to catholicize his subjects and merely added another decomposing ferment to the already existing ones. For, instead of winning over spiritually the Romanian people to his side, all that the Emperor's action succeeded in achieving was to divide it into two churches, the traditional Orthodox one and the newly created united one, favored by the rulers to the detriment of the first.

The inveterate opposition, offered by the privileged classes to all reforms initiated by the Emperor's authority, spoiled to a great extent the imperial program for improving the existing situation by suppressing unfair privileges and instituting a better and more impartial administration and brought about the paradoxical result that instead of the situation of the majority improving, it became much worse. For, following the revolt of the privileged classes under the leadership of Francis Rákoczi the Second against the centralization and Catholicization measures of the government, which actually imperiled for a moment the Emperor's domination over the recently conquered territories, the country had reached such a state of wretchedness, that it was imprudent to trouble it by radical reforms.

The Emperor, intimidated by the magnitude of that revolution, and owing to the dynastic plans to ensure the succession of the crown in the female line as well, and also to the defensive wars against the unceasing aggressiveness of Frederick the Second of Prussia, was forced to have recourse to the goodwill and help of the State organized political factors and to abandon his initial plan of reform and be content with half measures.

XXI

Internal Situations at the End of the Eighteenth Century, Joseph II, Horia's Revolution, and "Supplex Libellus Valachorum"

Respecting and maintaining the privileged structure of the State as it had developed during the time of Transylvanian principality of "the three nations' union" and of Verböczy's tripartite code of laws, the imperial government of Transylvania saw itself obliged to add to the already heavy existing taxes, which benefitted the privileged classes, also other new taxes needed for the keeping up of the huge apparatus of State. So that the Romanians, on whom all those taxes fell, had reached such a state of despair that they left their native land in masses crossing into Wallachia and Moldavia where, although the foreign government of the Phanariot Princes was also very oppressive, the situation was more bearable.

Neither all the innumerable edicts and imperial orders of the whole eighteenth century, nor the heavy punishments with which they threatened the families and fellow villagers of the fugitives, nor yet the strict control at the frontier or the promises of complete pardon for those who came back, not even the sanitary cordon and almost endemic epidemics of the plague in the Romanian Voivodeships, could stop the endless procession of emigrants leaving Transylvania secretly.

How could they do anything else but leave their homes when, as Count Auersperg, the Governor of Transylvania pointed out in his report of April 1st, 1772, addressed to Joseph II, son and co-regent of Maria Teresa, the peasants were forced even by the ordinance of 1769, which had improved somewhat the situation of the population, to give their feudal lords weekly "four days of manual labor and three days' work with beasts of draught." Besides, the peasants had to pay taxes, and also to keep out of their own lots the Government Officials whose "prevarications and malversations", more especially those of the tax collectors, they were made to feel very often.

Greatly worried by that state of things which proved that even in the new situation of international right, the internal organization and structure of Transylvania had remained approximately unchanged owing to the continuous opposition of the privileged "three nations", which everlastingly invoked their "constitutional liberties" at every attempt of reform on the part of the Government, the superior officials who had come from Vienna were often forced to appeal to the sovereign in order to remedy some of the too obvious evils. Amongst these Count Clary, in charge of the Treasury — the financial administration of the province — felt obliged to point out that "everything must be attempted to keep the Romanians who, though they were the poorest, were nevertheless the most numerous taxpayers in the country."

It is therefore not surprising that Joseph II, the monarch who represented most strikingly the centralist and absolutist tendencies of the Hapsburgs, should have been really horrified at the situation which he found in Transylvania, Banat, and the

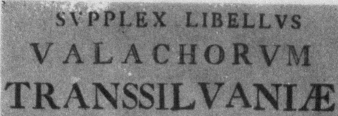

SVPPLEX LIBELLVS
VALACHORVM
TRANSSILVANIÆ
IVRA TRIBVS RECEPTIS NATIONIBVS COMMVNIA
POSTLIMINIO SIBI ADSERI
POSTVLANTIVM.

CVM NOTIS HISTORICO - CRITICIS
I. C. E.
CIVIS TRANSSILVANI.

CLAVDIOPOLI.

Sumptibus et Typis Martini Hochmeister, Cæsl. Reg. Dicast. Typographi & pr.
Bibliopolæ. MDCCXCI.

Supplex Libellus Valachorum

districts around the Tisa, in 1773, when he visited these countries.

He also was struck particularly by the foreign character of the ruling state compared to the population.

"I make it a duty of conscience, he wrote in a report addressed to the Council of State and to Empress Maria Teresa, his mother, to point out that this country, Transylvania, is indeed fine and beautiful but it is in need immediate help, and of radical reform, for neither improvement nor half measures suffice, the mentalities being already too spoiled. The governing classes are filled with a spirit of mistrust, suspicion, and intrigue. All of them are only interested in keeping their privileges, in not being hindered from collecting their incomes and in being free to do as they like with their underlings." More especially "the Hungarian nobility dreads nothing more in the world than anything that might lessen their incomes or restrict their rights which they extend fairly or foully as far as they possibly can, only to be able to exploit the peasants as much as they can."

"The peasant is a slave of his lord, he has no means whatever of subsistence, he must work much or little according to the good pleasure of his master, how and where the latter wishes. There can be no question of regulating the taxes" so that, concludes the emperor, "my conscience would prick me were I not to point out that this country more than any other needs laws establishing the taxes for the agricultural population."

The Emperor confirmed the truth of the reports sent to him by the superior officials already mentioned: Count Auersperg, who had stated "it has secretly come to my knowledge that whole villages are about to emigrate to Moldavia"; Count Clary who had also attracted attention to the fact that "if those evils are not curtailed soon, it is to be feared that whole districts, possibly many thousands of taxpayers, who have only been stopped until now from doing so by the war going on in Wallachia and Moldavia, will emigrate." He further added: "the unlimited work and cruel treatment which the holders of land mete out to their subjects are given as the principal motives for that emigration", for "the excesses go too far so that the peasant can no longer exist in such conditions."

In conclusion, the following conclusive and summarizing sentences of Emperor Joseph may be quoted: "these poor Romanian subjects, without doubt, the oldest and most numerous inhabitants of Transylvania, are tortured and treated unfairly by everybody, Hungarians and Saxons, so much that in truth, their fate when you know it is very much to be pitied and one can only wonder that there are still so many of them and that they have not all run away." And again: "It doesn't surprise me that their land is badly worked, for how could it be otherwise if you are not certain of keeping it from one day to another and have to work for the master every day and even every hour; how could the peasant, in such circumstances, attend to his land and do his best for it? As a matter of fact, the Romanians have spirit and their improvidence is most certainly the result of their misfortune, it enables them in case of need, when the situation becomes absolutely unbearable, to run away more easily into another country."

In face of such testimony even the leaders of the army in Vienna became alarmed and Count Lacy, President of the Imperial War Council, expressed the opinion that very drastic political measures should be taken. Those measures could only mean the abolition of "constitutional liberties" so dear to the privileged classes, for only by reforming the privilege structure of the whole organization of State was it possible to take from it that foreign character and cure the organic vices of which the whole country suffered, in all domains: economic, social, politic and national.

After he took over the government of the country, Joseph II tried to remedy those evils by abolishing the Transylvanian Constitution and by organizing the country on bases under his centralist ideas of "wise absolutism", in such a way that the whole apparatus of State should become the administrative instrument of the sovereign, capable of giving at last to the different regions of his great empire the consistency and unity it lacked. The intentions of the Emperor were sabotaged successfully by the privileged classes because, due to their too rationalistic and theoretical character, they did not correspond to local needs, and more especially because those privileged classes held all the commanding posts in the country's administration without which a country cannot do and the replacing of which takes time, one having to wait for a new generation to grow up in the spirit of those reforms.

Besides, the decreeing of German as the official language of the State confirmed once again its foreign character, so that all the good intentions embodied in the edict for religious tolerance, in the canceling of exemptions from taxpaying for the privileged, in the ordinances for the protection of the population and others, remained simple enunciations of principle, their execution being successfully prevented by those interested.

From the conflict which broke out between the sovereign and "the privileged nations", the Emperor came out defeated, being compelled as a result of the defeats suffered in his foreign policy and. in the unfortunate war against the Turks, to revoke on his deathbed all the measures he had passed during his reign.

The victim of the conflict however was, this time also, the Romanian population which, grateful for the kind and humane attitude which the Emperor had shown it during his repeated trips to Transylvania when he listened with interest to all complaints, and believing in his authority and power, rose in 1784 under the leadership of Nicolae Ursu, surnamed Horia — an intelligent peasant from Albac, a commune in the district Turda — to demand the application of the decreed measures.

As in the years 1437 and 1514, the unorganized peasant mobs were drowned in blood by the army of the privileged classes, more especially by that of the nobles, and the Emperor, occupied at that time with the project of exchanging his possessions in the Low Countries for Bavaria and being on the eve of war, had neither the intention nor the power to play the part of arbiter and to protect a population which had believed in and put its hopes in his intentions.

Butchered outside the town of Deva, the peasants scattered when the regular army of the State was turned on them too and their leaders, Horia and his two adjutants Cloşca and Crişan, were caught and executed at Alba Iulia, suffering the most atrocious martyrdom for the cause of social and national freedom; they were broken on the wheel and their bodies were maimed and torn in the presence of 2151 Romanian peasants, forced by the nobility's men to witness that horrible spectacle.

The fact that during the time of the revolt a strong current had formed among the peasants in favor of reconstructing the old Dacia, which they felt instinctively to be the only possibility

Horia

of giving back to the country its natural unity and them a political organization suitable to the natural requirements is not without significance.

After the repression of the rebellion and the death of the Emperor, the privileged classes, assembled at the Diet of Cluj in 1790, gave Transylvania a new constitutional order, which, as a matter of fact, was nothing but the reestablishment of the positions as they had been before the reign of Joseph II.

The new Emperor, Leopold II, under the impression of that defeat and feeling his power threatened also by the outbreak of the French revolution, was no longer inclined to recommence the struggles with the organized political forces in the country which had proved so stubborn but made up his mind to govern on the best terms with the privileged classes, to be able to face the imminent peril threatening from outside.

The Napoleon wars and the period of reaction which followed, dominated by the outstanding personality of Chancellor Metternich, transformed the State into an Austrian Empire and the most rabid upholder of the established privileged order, and most merciless adversary of all popular movements and political organization on an ethnic basis.

Hence it was only natural that during those decades the Romanian should remain in that same state of oppression by the three privileged "nations." Their attempts to get justice by legal means failed utterly but had the basic importance of having fixed in a political program their claims of national equality and social freedom.

The claims were formulated in a petition which they forwarded to the Emperor and which was called "Supplex

Libellus Valachorum Transsylvaniae." In it they asked that political and citizenship rights such as the privileged nations enjoyed should be restored to the Romanian people, that is to say, it should be recognized as being the "fourth nation" in the country's constitution, and that the Orthodox Church should also be accepted among the recognized religions. It also proposed that the Romanians should have a share — in proportion to the number of the population — in public functions and that general taxation be introduced for all the population in the country in proportion to the paying capacity of each one. The Emperor did not read the petition but sent it, just as his descendant Francis Joseph was to do a hundred years later with the "Memorandum" presented to him, to the Transylvanian privileged classes assembled in the Diet at Cluj, who turned it down with the same kind of indignation with which their autonomous Transylvanian Principality had forbidden the Romanian people to dare ever again to ask the Hungarian nobles to exempt them from having to work on holidays. So that the immediate effect of that petition was negative. Nor did the pleadings before the Transylvanian Diet of Bishop Ioan Inocenţiu Micu, Head of the Romanian United Church, in 1736, asking for the fulfillment of the promises which had been given when the Union had taken place, any more than the Romanian's politic Memorandum, in 1892, bring any immediate practical result. All the pleadings, interventions, and petitions of the Romanians remained unanswered, owing to the stubborn determination of the Hungarian privileged nobility not to yield one iota of their power.

Although it had no immediate consequences, the petition forwarded to Emperor Leopold II and refused by the privileged classes of Transylvania had nevertheless an epochal significance. For in that petition the things asked for are grounded on historical considerations, use having been made of the method employed with such success by the privileged classes for the maintenance of "their constitutional liberties."

In an epoch when arguments based on reason, humaneness, and justice were considered revolutionary and condemned as such at the very start, it was only possible to invoke arguments that could by their nature constitute a basis for discussion.

And as the only argument which the privileged classes could invoke to maintain the abnormal situations, created by their constitutional liberties, was of a so-called historical order, in the sense that privileged order was the inheritance of an ancient tradition of the State organization, there was no other way left to the Romanians to overturn that argument which had been accepted as valid, than to show that their claims were upheld by a historical right older and even better grounded.

The allusion to the Roman origin of the Romanian people, to its continuity, and to the priority of its existence before any of the other nations settled in these parts, conferred on the formulated claims their true character, that of a necessary historical reparation. That is why, feeling the solidity of the argument put forward, the Hungarian privileged classes contested and still contest today with much vehemence and passion the continuity of the Romanian people in Dacia, giving a controversy, scientific in nature, the character of a lawsuit which they plead with all the legal apparatus of permitted and non-permitted maneuvers and sophistication, in order to win the acceptance of the world's public opinion.

At the same time, the demands made in the petition constituted also an attempt to give a positive solution, within the policy of continuity adopted by the sovereign, to the thorny problem of organizing the whole Danubian basin within the Unitarian framework of the Austrian Empire, giving its structure of State a more natural character, more autochthonous, more corresponding to the rooted requirements of these regions.

So that the petition of the Romanians wished to eliminate the foreign and superficial character from the privileged forms of the State organization, in order to give them the necessary ethnic content which could take from them their anachronic immobility and give them the possibility of a normal evolution in concordance with time.

XXII

The Character of Romanian Patriotism
and Hungarian Imperialism

For the Romanian people, however, that petition has a still greater significance, for it expressed a state of conscience decisive for all its subsequent development. It succeeded in emerging from the vicissitudes and misfortunes of the past and in attaining through its spiritual aptitudes and cultural creations the conscience of its historical destiny, of its origin and ethnical unity.

Dominated by that conscience it fulfilled in a harmonious correlation its cultural mission and its political, social, and national claims. Through the learned works of its scholars of the seventeenth, of the latter half of the eighteenth and the beginning of the nineteenth centuries, that conscience was formed and afterwards spread by wise teachers all over the Romanian countries, in Transylvania, in Banat, in the districts near the Tisa, in the Maramureş of its ancient voivodes and in the Romanian Principalities, in Moldavia and Wallachia, where it became so deeply rooted that it was able to produce an all-powerful current of national renaissance, cultural creation, social pacification and political organization and realization, expressed in the successive stages of: the union of the Principalities, the distribution of lands to the peasants, the freeing from slavery of the gypsies (tziganes) between 1859-1866, the declaration of its independence and its raising to a Kingdom in the international order, its internal progress and consolidation during the reign of the great King Carol I, between the years 1877 and 1916 and finally, the including after World War I under the glorious reign of King Ferdinand the Loyal, of the neighboring regions on both sides of the Carpathians inhabited by Romanians, within the natural geographical framework of the present day State.

Hence, it can be affirmed without exaggeration that the present State and national conscience of the Romanian people is the hard won result of its civilizing capacity, while the Hungarian State and its revisionist claims are nothing but the expression of an instinct to dominate and oppress, produced by the privileged and foreign character of its political institutions. The formula going the rounds which characterizes Hungary as being the last feudal state in Europe is neither inappropriate nor groundless.

XXIII

Conditions at the Beginning of the Nineteenth Century

That is why Hungary has always formed a discordant note in the generous currents of political emancipation and social reform which have dominated Europe during the last century, falsifying their contents and using them as a screen behind which it could continue freely its work of oppressing and exploiting the neighboring nations in the Danubian basin. So that towards the end of the absolutist epoch, the Hungarian nobility of all categories began a violent campaign of agitations in the diet and in "country assemblies" — those autonomous assemblies of the privileged which ruled over a district — to impose Hungarian instead of Latin as the official language for all public manifestations, with the intention of giving to the polyglot State an aspect of unity which it lacked and of smothering the nationality of other ethnical individualities.

The opposition of the Romanians, Slovaks, Germans, Croatians, and Ruthenians was fought with the greatest violence by the privileged Hungarian classes, in the name of the liberal ideology which was gaining more and more ground in the civilized countries of Europe.

The representative figure for all these efforts remains the great agitator Louis Kossuth who, although he set himself up to be the champion of the most advanced ideas of that time, did not hesitate to declare that the "Magyarization of the Croatians, Romanians, and Saxons" would have to be sped up "or else we are fated to disappear."

For he realized that if a centralized administration were obtained in Budapest, a Unitarian Hungarian Government for the whole of that region, an army of their own, and the institution of an assessment electoral regime, all other reforms would remain merely enunciations of principles good to win friendships abroad, but without any practical value.

Indeed what good could come to the population from the abolition of the privileged order and the feudal system of serfdom, if, based on the high census of the electoral regime, the domination remained merely under a changed aspect still in the possession of the old privileged classes, and from the permission to buy oneself out of vassalage, if the peasants owing to the state of oppression and poverty in which they did not have the means to make use of that theoretical right.

The ancestral instincts of domination over other nations were, on the other hand, to be richly satisfied by the inclusion of Transylvania and of the districts near the Tisa in the organization of the Hungarian State, and inclusion which was clamored for by both the Radicals and the Moderates, because, as Stephan Ludwig Roth — a Saxon pastor from Transylvania, who soon after was to become a martyr for his generous ideas, being executed in 1848 by the revolutionary regime of "the liberal" Kossuth — stated, Transylvania was Romanian. "Transylvania," said he in the year 1842, when the Diet assembled in Cluj was busily discussing the introduction of the Hungarian language as the official language, "had long since been having naturally a language belonging to the country,

Stephen Ludwig Roth

which was neither German nor Hungarian, but the Romanian language. The only language which is current all over the country" he emphasized, "is the Romanian language," pointing out that there was no object in denying a truth recognized, at the bottom, by all consciences. On the contrary, he went on, speaking to the Hungarian nobility, it is necessary to give to the Romanians "the food of justice and the cooling drink of a humane treatment", "to respect their dignity as human beings and honor their Christian faith, to give them the possibility of an independent life and means of education", and he finished up with the prophetic words: "take heed what you do and do not throw with criminal daring living coal on dry straw. You are sowing wind and you will reap a hurricane."

XXIV

Revolution of 1848,
Consequences of Hungarian Egoism

The hurricane broke out in truth in the year 1848 when Louis Kossuth, making use of the general movement of political emancipation, instituted the independent Hungarian republic under his leadership, to violate the existence of the other peoples and, penetrating with his armies into Transylvania, began the most bloody and inhuman war against the nations of those regions. By thus disorganizing completely the whole Danubian basin, Kossuth provoked by his action the intervention and invasion of the Russian army of occupation, fulfilling the prophecy which Count Szécheny, his more clearsighted compatriot had made one year before, namely that Kossuth would "lead the Hungarian people into such an impasse that the Lord himself would no longer be able to extract them."

The Hungarians did not listen either to the pathetic appeal of their great patriot Baron Wesselényi, who, although blind, attended the Diet and spoke as follows about the Romanians: "The future is blacker than the darkness of my eyes. Only peace and understanding can save us. Stephen the Saint used to tell his son: happy the countries that have numerous peoples. That advice which our notables have taken to heart weighs on us like a curse, for the peoples are wicked and rise one against the other.

The Romanians deserve special sympathy, and they must not be refused that name, for it really is true that they are the descendants of the Romans. It is to their interest also to meet us for, like us, they are isolated in these parts."

But Kossuth and the privileged classes of the Hungarian nobility in the Transylvanian Diet disposed of the Romanians without listening to them, and terrorizing them with the formula "Union or Death", brought in by force the decreeing of "The Union of Transylvania with Hungary."

The Romanians however, at a large popular meeting held on the field of "Liberty" near Blaj, proclaimed their wish for a national life of their own and the right to control their own fate.

Upon the Saxon deputies retiring also from the Transylvanian Diet in a sign of protest against the decreed union, Transylvania was invaded by the armies of the Hungarian Government and the armed mobs of the Hungarian nobility. Nevertheless, the Romanians and Saxons tried to arrive at an understanding with the invaders, forming for that purpose a Peace Committee, the aim of which could not be attained owing to Kossuth's intransigence.

As a matter of fact, Csány, the delegate of the Hungarian Government for the administration of Transylvania, defined as follows in a public manifesto the attitude of the revolutionary regime: "You poor Wallachians, disappointed and led astray by the intriguing of Austrian officers. There is no remembrance whatever either in man or history of any free national life so far as you are concerned. You were slaves under the Romans, slaves of the nomad peoples, slaves also for the last thousand years, only the Hungarians will help you glimpse the dawn of freedom." Immediately after which, almost in the same breath, they promised them if they did not submit, "the corporal punishment which their crimes deserve." These crimes consisted in resistance crowned with success, which their army of peasant-volunteers under the leadership of a few chosen tribunes, namely Avram Iancu, Buteanu, and Axente Sever, were opposing to the Hungarian invasion and to the atrocities which they committed, preventing the extension of the Hungarian conquest to Bihor and Sătmar, that is to say to the regions on the present Western frontier of Romania. Because, as Kossuth himself put it in a letter addressed to Nicolae Bălcescu, the Romanian historian and patriot who was making yet another effort, as a go between, to promote an understanding between the Romanians and the Hungarians, he could only conceive the liberty of the Romanians in the following manner: "your liberty will be the scaffold, your claim of equal rights will mean that the peoples who share the country with the Hungarians will have to be absorbed by the Hungarian element."

As a consequence, not even the armistice which had been signed because of a future understanding was respected, the Hungarians, having arrested without warning many of the Romanian leaders, hanged Buteanu the prefect of Zarand, did away with Dobra, and assassinated even Dragoş who had been tireless in his efforts to promote an understanding.

In truth the points of view could never agree, for in face of the Hungarian tendencies of domination and oppression, the Romanians aimed u as they explained in their petition of 28 December 1848 — at reforming the Empire into a "constitutional monarchy in which all the nations were to have a share." Deeply conscious of their responsibility for order in the Danubian basin, whose ethnical expression they represented in these parts, they

Avram Iancu

even expressed the wish in the petition presented on 25 February 1848, by the Metropolitan Şaguna to Emperor Francis Joseph at Olmütz, of "the union of all Romanians in the Austrian State as an independent nation under the Austrian scepter", under the Emperor who would have become "Great Duke of the Romanians."

So that while the Hungarians were provoking disorganization and anarchy in the South-East of Europe by their selfish particularism and tendencies of national oppression, the Romanians were planning to ensure in those regions a more stable balance by a cooperation between the peoples interested, within a federalist form of State.

It was just that cooperation likely to assure peace and a natural balance for the so sorely tried regions of the Danubian basin, that the Hungarians did not want to be realized at any price, for then they would have had to confine themselves to their ethnic territory and renounce their wishes of domination and oppression over other peoples.

Exiled after the fall of his regime of revolutionary oppression, and under the influence of his new surroundings of Anglo-Saxon freedom and equity, Kossuth had to recognize also, too late however to have any effect, that the only possibility of improving the conditions in those parts was the recognition and respecting of the various national individualities, for it was only on that natural foundation that a consolidated state of order could be built, which he now visualized as a confederacy of the nations interested.

XXV

Hungarian Particularism Prevents
the Reconstruction of Central Europe

But although his revolutionary regime had fallen, his scheme of oppression continued to dominate the spirit and actions of his co-nationals who had remained in the country, under the authority, re-enthroned .by the Russian bayonets, of imperial Austrian absolutism.

For the Hungarian privileged classes, Kossuthism in its revolutionary form remained for all its defeat and despite the disaster, it provoked, the guiding light of all their political action. Realizing at long last that at least the outward forms of their policy would have to be changed, that it was no longer possible to maintain openly a privileged constitution and a feudal system amid a world that was fervently upholding the creed of national liberty and social justice, the Hungarian privileged nobles recognized in the leading ideas of the defeated revolutionary government their only chance of saving for themselves their old power, under the disguise of the new liberal ideas. Of course, the ideas themselves did not interest them at the very least, but merely the possibility they offered of allowing them to retain their domination over non-Hungarian nations. For that reason, they did not hesitate to accept even an absolutist Government and to oppose stubbornly a constitutional one that did not satisfy their wishes.

The explanation of that attitude, seemingly so strange, did not escape the deep insight of an experienced contemporary observer. In a report dated October 12, 1861, forwarded by A. A. Paton, British consul at Lübeck to Sir A. Layard, Secretary of State at the Foreign Office, we find the following characteristic passage: "I have serious doubts as to Austria's constitutional experiment, for the Hungarians will continue to play the game of the absolutist party by their unacceptable demands. They did the same thing already in 1848 — 1849, seeking to obtain an independent government and army and they do it again today. Austria however will not be able to maintain herself with two imperial legislative chambers which are solitary and hostile at the same time."

"The Hungarians have paid their contributions to Schwarzenberg and his centralized, bureaucratic and military absolutism and refuse to pay them to Schmerling and his constitutional unity and provincial autonomy, which shows that they knew that a real honest constitutional government would be more fatal to their domination over non-Hungarian populations than absolutism itself."

Their attitude, so vividly described in that report, was indeed one of systematic sabotaging of all attempts to reconstruct the State on more healthy and natural bases, and of watching and waiting for the opportune moment to realize their "unacceptable" demands, in order to extend their oppression over the other peoples and more especially over Transylvania and the Romanian people, by putting into practice the same methods as Kossuth's revolutionary government had made use of for a short time.

XXVI
The Austro-Hungarian Dualism of 1867:
Consequences of Forced Magyarization

The opportune moment arrived at last in 1866, when the victories of the Prussian Kingdom governed by Bismarck drove the Austrian Empire to the verge of bankruptcy. During that serious crisis, the Hungarians kept in touch with the outside enemy, as they had done so many times before in the course of their historical existence, more markedly in 1791, when the Hungarian privileged nobles in conjunction with Prussia fostered revolts within the country.

The danger of a Hungarian rebellion after a long period of veiled hostility seemed again imminent to the Emperor. Demoralized by the defeat he had suffered and by the loss of his personal prestige, anxious to obtain the active help of the stubborn Hungarian nobles for the necessary reconstruction of the State, and influenced also by his wife Elizabeth, whom Count Andrassy had won over to the Hungarian cause, Emperor Francis Joseph abandoned this attempt at federalism, begun by granting to the peoples within the absolutist State a wider provincial autonomy and fairer national liberties, and decided at last with great reluctance to satisfy the demands of the gentlemen from Budapest which — expressed in very respectful terms — Francis Deák had laid before him.

By the enthronement of the new constitutional order, the State was given a new character, that of a dual monarchy, the Empire being divided into two halves, with two parliaments and two different governments; with different legal codes and with two different economic systems and different customs posts. Numerous peoples in the monarchy passed under the preponderant German element, on one side, and under the harsh domination of the Hungarian privileged classes, on the other. Only the person of the monarch, the foreign policy, and the army remained common to both countries and stood for the unity of the State.

The new dual monarchy was the most abnormal and most fatal of all possible solutions, for it meant in fact the beginning of the end of the State's existence. The Hungarians did not look upon that solution as an achieved end but as an opportunist solution, their object being the simple personal union of two completely different states or even the complete independence of their extensive Kingdom, which they had obtained in a moment of panic through conspiracies, threats and bedroom intrigues. Right from the very beginning, even from the institution of those new forms of state, the Hungarian privileged classes, having secured the exclusive possession of the desired factors for domination, directed the political action of the Hungarian Kingdom, guiding it — under the deceiving disguise of a liberal and parliamentary organization, which, however, was really directed behind the scenes by their club of nobles called the "National House" — towards the realization of the aims which Louis Kossuth had shown them during his short revolutionary regime.

Hence they aimed at a progressive undermining of the central authority, at seizing the supreme government and using it — even concerning foreign policy — for their own selfish ends, and at the compulsory Magyarization of the nations left prey to their ruthless domination, causing thus the outbreak of the harsh and ceaseless conflict between the peoples of the Empire, known all over the world under the suggestive title of the "war of nations", which deprived the State of the peace necessary for its internal consolidation and the South-East of Europe of the balance and stableness which is needed in the general interest of peace and civilization.

The final result of Kossuth's government had been disorganization and anarchy in the Danubian basin, followed by the penetration of the Russian armies into those parts; the natural result of the creation of the Hungarian Kingdom within the framework of the Dual Monarchy was the outbreak of the World War in 1914, and the institution of a Communist dictatorship in Budapest in 1919, with the states of crisis, insecurity, and wretchedness which it provoked.

A whole series of family tragedies: the execution of the Monarch's brother, Archduke Maximilian, who had become Emperor of Mexico, the suicide of Archduke Rodolphe, his son and heir to the throne, the assassination of his wife, Empress Elizabeth, the serious misunderstandings, conflicts and renouncements in the Imperial family, was added to the troubles of government and helped to destroy the Sovereign's power of initiative and decision. Sadly disappointed in life, even doubtful that the State he governed could survive, and having lost all faith in reforms and hopes of any future improvement in the situation, he took refuge in a frightened passivity and fruitless opposition to any attempt which might have changed ever so little the abnormal character of the Dual Monarchy. Under the permanent pressure of the insatiable lust for domination of the

Hungarian privileged classes and their governments, Francis Joseph committed all the acts of ingratitude, renegation and betrayal it is possible for a monarch to commit. He consented to make peace with his victorious enemy, with Prussia, to follow in the wake of Bismarck and to become the docile tool of the international policy pursued by the new German Empire which, by its economic and military power, made possible the Hungarian State's policy of national oppression.

He pursued a policy of expansion and menace about the neighboring countries in the Balkan Peninsula, he abandoned and forfeited the trust of the peoples in his country who had put their faith in him and even fought for him, causing that state of strained tension which resulted in the catastrophe of the last war.

Only once the emperor dared to oppose Hungarian wishes when exceeding all limits, they demanded the sacrifice of the last element of cohesion, by wanting an army of their own for their half of the State. Then it was that the abnormity and fragility of that State were made obvious, for, in face of the threat to introduce the universal vote which would have deprived their Kingdom at one go of its imposed Hungarian character, the interested ruling classes immediately renounced their demands.

To make up for this they permitted themselves every kind of abuse, injustice, and oppression towards the peoples which the Emperor had so unexpectedly handed back to their unhampered rule. As in the time of Kossuth, the ruling classes of the Hungarian Kingdom did not follow the advice of the moderate party, which realized that to keep the State from collapsing an understanding with the other peoples who dwelt there — obtainable by a minimum of concessions — was absolutely

necessary. The law of nations was drawn up for the eyes of the
World to see, but remained a dead letter and never was applied
in a single case. Francis Deák, its author, surnamed "the nation's
wise man" because he had succeeded in getting the Emperor's
consent for the dual form of state, remained isolated,
overwhelmed with flattering words but without influence, the
power passing to men who had no scruples or problems of
conscience, and who embodied better and more truly the aims
of the ruling classes. The governing classes composed of the
Hungarian nobility of the former privileged classes, to which
were added the docile class of the State paid officials and that of
the well-to-do population of recent origin in Budapest and a few
other largish towns, created by the artificial means of the State
policy, continued with the ardent fervor of neophytes the
traditional policy of intolerance and egoism of the privileged
classes who had preceded them, that is to say, the policy of
national persecution, social oppression, and economic
exploitation of the former feudal lords, transformed now into
large estate owners, heads of enterprises and statesmen who
masked their primary instincts under the deliberately assumed
outer aspect of an Anglo-Saxon way of living.

Their hatred and persecution were mainly directed against
Transylvania and the Romanian people, who remained
unshaken in their determination to preserve their ethnic
character and the astonishing power of resistance of their robust
peasant nature. The imposing personality of the Metropolitan
Şaguna had even succeeded in raising that power of resistance
in the short period of relative liberty of the years preceding the
dualism, giving it in the organic statute of the Orthodox Church
based on the principle of order in freedom, forms of its own and
suitable for the safeguarding of the most vital national and

Metropolitan Andrei Şaguna

spiritual interests. The Romanian people soon found out what it could expect from the government of the country when, in the Parliament at Budapest, the request of the few Romanian deputies for equal rights for the Romanian people was answered with the threat of putting into execution the same method of extermination as that which had been employed in America by the Conquistadores against the Red Indians. Coloman Tisza, the Prime Minister himself, speaking to them used the elegant and significant words: "Shut up and pay." Under such conditions and after the voting of the new electoral law which made impossible the election of non-Hungarian deputies disapproved by the Government, as not even 6% of the population could now vote — in Transylvania only 3,2% as compared to 6,5 — 7,5% in the middle of the Pannonian plain — the Romanian people were obliged to assume the mute attitude of protest of political passivity. During that time, from 1875 to 1906, the ruling classes were able to act as despotically as they pleased without it being possible to lay complaint against them before any authorized forum.

By laws muzzling the Press, the Kindergarten Act, elementary and secondary teaching, by the way, the juries were selected, by administrative pressure, by the Magyarization of names, by terror and corruption, in a word by all and every means; they tried to Magyarize the Romanians and other nations, "by fire and sword", by "their systematic degradation and by their political, moral and economical decadence."

Insults were heaped on a memorandum from the university students of free Romania, which tried to show to the public opinion of the world the unimaginable oppression endured by the Romanians in Hungary, and the memorial drawn up in 1892 by the National Romanian Party and addressed to the Crown, in which the grievances of the Romanian people were expounded was sent back unopened, the delegation of 300 persons that took it to Vienna not being even received by Francis Joseph. Perhaps even that action of unheard-of contempt for a whole people might have passed unnoticed if the Hungarian Government due to its exaggerated chauvinism had not had the imprudence to bring action into the bargain against the authors of that unconsidered petition and — through revoltingly biased jury — to bring sentences of imprisonment varying from 5 years to 2 months, altogether 40 years of imprisonment for 14 people. Not content with this, the authorities instigated the Hungarian population at Turda to devastate completely the residence of the Romanian leader, Dr. Ioan Raţiu, when he returned home from the trial so that he was able to say: "Thank you, Gentlemen, that is just what you are like and what I have always known you to be like." The unexpected repercussion of that unfair trial in all the civilized world was one of unanimous revolt. G. Clemenceau gave it expression at the time by the following lapidary phrases, so characteristic of his temperament. "A trial of high treason is going on at the present moment in Cluj, the capital of Transylvania, which interests to the highest point both the subjects of Emperor Francis Joseph and all those who wish for a better distribution of justice among peoples. The Romanians have right on their side. It is not a big word but the Hungarians have made a big affair of it."

The Hungarian Governments however did not allow themselves to be influenced either by the opinion of foreign countries or by the courteous and friendly interventions of King Carol I of Romania at the court of Emperor Francis Joseph. Their instincts of oppression made them deaf to any advice of moderation. On the contrary in the years that followed, under

Leaders of the Memorandum Movement in Transylvania

the governments dominated by the limitless fanaticism and stubborn energy of Count Stephen Tisza, the measures of persecution and oppression gained in intensity in all fields. Internal unstableness and the wretched condition of the population grew however in the same proportion, for not the strongest will in the world can violate natural conditions with impunity, without fatal consequences. As in the eighteenth century, the abnormal situations at the end of the nineteenth century and the beginning of the present one showed themselves in an ever-growing wave of emigration of the population to foreign countries, especially to the United States, revealing thus to wide circles uninfluenced by any political creed or national preference, the real situation in Hungary. Thus, for example, in a monograph on the life of Albert Ballin, the manager of the German Navigation Company, Hamburg America Linie, we find the following illuminating passage: "The constantly growing emigration from the Hungarian part of the Habsburg monarchy subjected to an unfortunate agrarian constitution, has attracted the attention of the Hungarian Government circles. Hungary's pride can bear that sons of hers, degraded to real helots on the lands of great landowners, should leave the country, but she wants these thousands of emigrants from Hungary to turn their back on their native land from a Hungarian port." As a consequence, the Hungarian Government proposed to the two German navigation companies to create a subventioned line at Fiume, which they refused to do because it was not profitable enough. The Cunard Line accepted the Hungarian proposal; the German navigation companies signed then a cooperation contract with the Austro-American Company of Trieste, as a result of which the rivalry of the two principal ports of the Dual Monarchy became more marked.

The Hungarian oppression, while showing that it had repercussions also on the far off problems of the maritime rivalries of before World War I, revealed at the same time both the organic vices of the organization of State and the unreal spirit of limitless megalomania which filled its governing circles, making them incapable of understanding and of finding a solution for the real and the gravest problems of State. That morbid megalomania often took the most grotesque forms, the atavistic instinct of domination of its governing classes flaunting its contempt for the country's population provoking even the ironic surprise of disinterested observers. An example of that phenomenon is found in the Memoirs of the Austrian statesman Baernreither, published in Vienna after his death in 1928. The entry for 1 January 1913 is as follows: "Yesterday I talked with Prince Fürstenberg who is about to return to his post in Bucharest. He is optimistic with regards to Romania and hopes that the Liberal Party also will side with the Triple Alliance if Tisza could be convinced to treat the Romanians in Hungary differently from the way he has been doing, that is to say, to give them officials of their own nationality and to ensure for them a better situation by electoral reform. Fürstenberg did his best to establish relations between Tisza and the Romanian leaders in the Hungarian Parliament. His efforts did not scorn the settlement of the very smallest detail and he tried to convince Tisza to acknowledge the greeting of the Romanian deputies." At that time Prince Fürstenberg was the plenipotentiary minister of the Austro-Hungarian Monarchy in Bucharest.

XXVII

Decomposition of the Dual Monarchy
was Inevitable

The refusal of the Hungarian Prime Minister to acknowledge the greeting of the legal representatives of the Romanian people is embodied in a gesture of defiance all the lack of consideration of the legal state for the Romanian people that had been given into his hand: it reveals the irreconcilable divorce between the artificial organization of State and the living and natural facts. Hence it was only natural that the State should not be able to last very much longer under such circumstances.

One cannot know whether the attempt at the eleventh hour of Archduke Francis Ferdinand, the heir to the throne, would have been successful. He had planned that on taking over the throne he would give the monarchy a more natural and lasting foundation, by transforming it into a federative State composed of the nations that formed the monarchy.

Judging from past experiences, its chances of success were extremely few. For the tragic fall of all the ruling forms of State in these regions in the course of history, was due to the fact that they did not express ethnical realities and the real needs of the country. That is the reason why the element which had been created to uphold the State, namely the privileged classes, became transformed into proven factors of dissolution and disintegration. It was they who brought about the fall of the medieval Hungarian Kingdom, due to them the Habsburg domination was unable to consolidate itself neither in an absolutist, federalist, constitutional or dual form.

The murder of Archduke Francis Ferdinand at Sarajevo, in 1914, gave its death blow in any case to the last attempt made to give the Danubian basin the peace and stableness it needed, by reforming the existing organization.

After the failure of all the attempts made, there remained only one possibility, namely that of giving the Danubian basin at long last, an order founded on totally different bases, on the real possibilities of its natural regions. There remained only the solution which the First World War gave it by constituting the national states.

Even those who had the greatest interest to prevent it had to bow in the face of the verdict of history. Count Ottokar Czernin, one of the last Foreign Ministers of the fallen empire, who had fought right up to the last for the maintenance of the Dual Monarchy, was compelled to recognize with resignation, in his memoirs published immediately after the signing of peace, that "the hour of the Austro-Hungarian Monarchy had struck" and to confess with grief that today — that is to say at the time when the peace was being signed — "it was his conviction that the decomposition of the Monarchy would have taken place even without the war."

Maps

SCHEME OF THE DIRECTIONS THE HUNGARIAN INVASIONS FOLLOWED IN THE DANUBIAN BASIN

Directions of the Hungarian invasions

THE DACIAN EXPANSION ANNEX No. 2

From *Constantin C. Giurescu*, «Istoria Românilor», vol. I

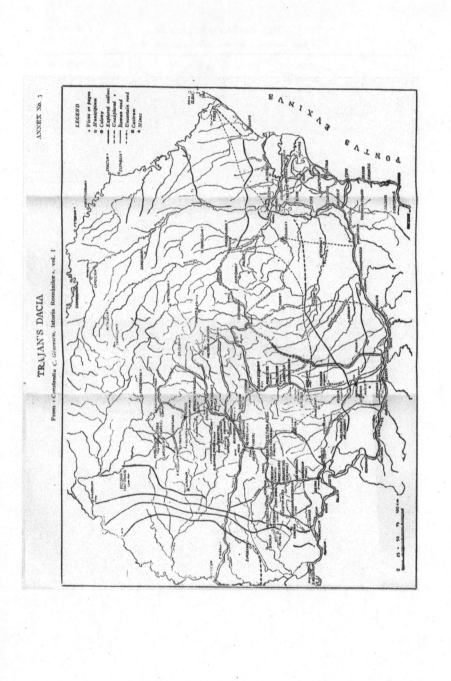

ANNEX No. 3

TRAJAN'S DACIA

From « Constandin C. Giurescu, Istoria Românilor », vol. I

MAP OF THE SLAVO-RUMANIAN VOIVODESHIPS AND OF THE PRINCIPAL LOCALITIES MENTIONED BY THE ANONYMOUS NOTARY'S CHRONICLE

From G. Popa-Lisseanu, « Izvoarele Istoriei Românilor », vol. I

LEGEND

f. = Flumen
S. = Sylva
C. = Castrum
M. = Montes
St. = Stagnum

THE DANUBIAN BASIN FROM 1526 TO 1699

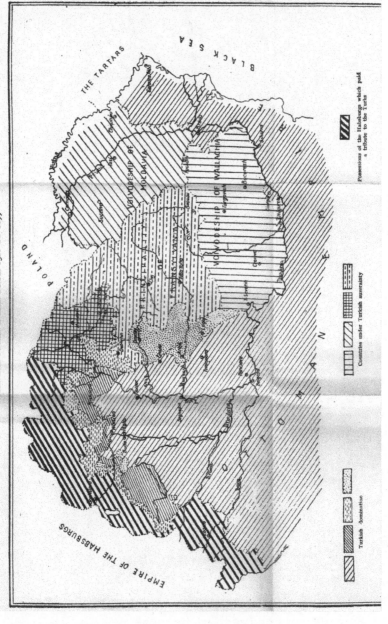

POLAND

THE TARTARS

BLACK SEA

EMPIRE OF THE HABSBURGS

VOIVODESHIP OF MOLDAVIA

TRANSYLVANIA
PRINCIPALITY

VOIVODESHIP OF WALLACHIA

OTTOMAN EMPIRE

Possessions of the Habsburgs which paid a tribute to the Turks

Countries under Turkish suzerainty

Turkish domination

Index

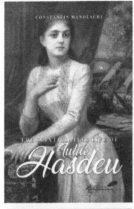
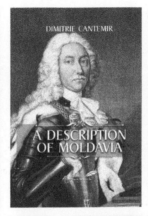